PRAYER MOVES GOD

Dedication

I would like to thank the Lord Jesus Christ for saving us. I would like to thank the Father for sending Him. I would like to thank the Holy Spirit for coming and remaining here with us – Sealing us unto the Day of Redemption.

A special thanks to my wife – Rosa. I love you – you are my girl!

Remember – Prayer is a daily necessity for daily triumph!

Table of Contents

Introduction 5

Chapter 1 7
  What is Prayer? 7

Chapter 2 14
  The Dominion Mandate 14

Chapter 3 32
  Revival Fires 32
    John Knox 37
    Evan John Roberts 39
    William Seymour 42
    John Hyde 48
    The Prayers of Sir Winston Churchill's Intercessor 51
    Rees Howell 53
    Battle of Dunkirk 57
    Fasts Proclaimed in American History 62
    National Days of Prayer and Fasting – Great Britain 66

Chapter 4 69
  The Prayers of Abraham 69

Chapter 5 83
  The Prayers of Moses 83

Chapter 6 91
  The Prayers of Elijah 91

Chapter 7 104
  The Prayers of Esther 104

Chapter 8 128
  The Prayers of Daniel 128

Chapter 9 140
Activating Angelic Ministry 140

Chapter 10 150
The Prayers of our Lord Jesus Christ 150
He Rose Up Early to Pray 151
Before His Baptism He Prayed 153
During His Forty Day Fast 153
Jesus Habit of Prayer 155
The Transfiguration 156
The Garden of Gethsemane 157
Jesus is Our Intercessor 158

Chapter 11 162
Praying Strategic Prayers 162
The Infernal Kingdom 177
Principalities 178
The Powers 184
Rulers of Darkness 187
Spiritual Host of Wickedness 189
The Eyes of Your Understanding 191

Chapter 12 195
Covenant Prayer Keys 195
Abide in Him – The Key to Answered Prayer 196
The Prayer of Faith 203
Corporate Prayer 207
The Prayer of Agreement 210

Chapter 13 217
Decreeing and Declaring...217
Declarations..217
Decrees 219

Introduction

"Prayer is a daily necessity for daily triumph." – **Archbishop Nicholas Duncan-Williams**

The most important lesson we can learn in life is how to pray. We must learn how to pray so that our prayers get God's attention. The person who has done the most impactful and consistent praying is the most immortal because prayers don't die. Prayers outlive the lives of those who uttered them. The lips that uttered them may be closed in death and the heart that felt them may have ceased to beat; but prayers live on before God and God's heart is set on them.

In this exciting encounter with prayer, you will receive fresh insight and revelation from God's Word on the purpose, power, and supremacy of prayer and I know that, as a result, every dimension of your life will be absolutely transformed and the destiny of generations yet unborn will be tremendously impacted. As you embark on this adventure of discovery of spiritual truth – there will be a release of supernatural keys that will cause an impartation of a strong prayer anointing that has been drawn out of decades of consistent prayer and spiritual warfare.

Prophetically, I know that God is raising a new breed of intercessors and prayer warriors that will enforce God's will for many generations. The destiny of cities, nations, and continents are birthed by the prayers of God's people. The prayers of God's people are the capital block in heaven by which Christ carries out His great work here on earth. The earth is changed and revolutionized. Angels powerfully move by might and God's agenda is enforced when the prayers of His people are more numerous and more efficient.

Nothing happens until someone prays. God can do nothing for humanity until someone prays! Prayer is the highest calling above every other calling. This is the time for you to rise up and take your place in His presence for the establishment of divine purpose. This is the time for you to go beyond the veil and enter into the heavenly holy of holies by the blood of the lamb to enforce prophetic decrees over nations and continents. God is counting on you and the whole earth is groaning and waiting for the manifestation of the sons of God!

Chapter 1

What is Prayer?

*"God does nothing but in answer to prayer; and even they who have been converted to God, without praying for it themselves (which is exceeding rare), were not without the prayers of others. Every new victory which a soul gains is the effect of a new prayer." – **John Wesley***

The call to prayer is the Father's invitation to enter into His presence. It is the Father's invitation into the throne room. Prayer is the voice of faith to the Father. Prayer is the Living Word on the lips of faith. Prayer gives a voice to our needs.

Let us therefore come boldly unto the throne of grace that we may obtain mercy and find grace to help in a time of need. (Hebrews 4:16)

Prayer allows us to come boldly into the Throne Room of the Father to receive illumination and advanced knowledge to pray, as we ought to. Prayer is our ability to stand in the gap and intercede for nations, cities, communities, churches, leaders, families, and ordinary people so that the will of God can be enforced over and above the plans of the enemy.

In the beginning, there was no need for prayer. Man had unrestricted communion and fellowship with God. Man spoke and whatever he said was established. He named the animals and the woman with final authority. Whatever man needed, God knew beforehand and supplied even before man asked. He provided a garden, four rivers, substance for food and companionship. Man had dominion.

Making our requests known to God allows us to experience the manifestation of God in our lives as well as discover what He is capable of doing. Prayer is a tool and a weapon, which is available to anyone in Christ; in prayer we discover the authority of the Name of Jesus and how to use it. We embrace the ability of the One dwelling in us and we receive a revelation of our rights and privileges in Christ. This is the reason why Christ said:

"….men ought always to pray and not to faint." (Luke 18:1b)

In the parable in Luke 18, Jesus Christ was emphasizing the need for continuous, persistent prayer based on faith. Prayer has to become a part of our daily lifestyle.

Prayer is also an opportunity to fellowship and commune with God. Your prayer life creates intimacy with God. During these times, you have the opportunity to pour out your heart to God and God also has the opportunity to reveal His plans and purposes to you. Prayer is a time when divinity meets with humanity for the fulfillment of divine purposes.

Call unto me, and I will answer thee, and shew thee great and mighty things, which thou knowest not. (Jeremiah 33:3)

Apostle Paul said in 1 Corinthians 16:9 "For a great door AND effectual is opened unto me, and there are many adversaries." Open doors always attract enemies. The door can open, but in order for you to enter and be effective, you will need to deal with your adversaries. Such as anti-progress forces, all forms of sabotage and demonic interference. It is by prayer that we defend our position and enter through the open door. We have keys in prayer!

Peter gets a revelation from the Father of who Christ is and the Lord releases the keys to the kingdom.

And it came to pass, as he was alone praying, his disciples were with him: and he asked them, saying, Whom say the people that I am? They answering said, John the Baptist; but some say, Elias; and others say, that one of the old prophets is risen again. He said unto them, But whom say ye that I am? Peter answering said, The Christ of God. (Luke 9:18-20)

An extended version of this interaction is in Matthew 16:16-19:

And Simon Peter answered and said, Thou art the Christ, the Son of the living God. And Jesus answered and said unto him, Blessed art thou, Simon Barjona: for flesh and blood hath not revealed it unto thee, but my Father which is in heaven. And I say also unto thee, That thou art Peter, and upon this rock I will build my church; and the gates of hell shall not prevail against it. And I will give unto thee the keys of the kingdom of heaven: and whatsoever thou shalt bind on earth shall be bound in heaven: and whatsoever thou shalt loose on earth shall be loosed in heaven.

Jesus was praying for the disciples in Luke 9:18 after a great miracle had been performed. The miracle of the fish and loaves was a benchmark in the life of the disciples; because they had for the first time, not just been observers of the Kingdom, but had directly participated in the miracle of the fish and loaves. Jesus in praying asked the Father to give them illumination. Peter responded and identified correctly the revelation of who Christ is. This is the revelation Jesus said He would use to build His Church. The prayers of Jesus gave Peter access to the throne room to receive revelation from the Father about who Jesus is. After Peter received the Revelation, Jesus gave him the keys of the Kingdom of Heaven to bind and to loose.

The keys to bind and loose are very important in intercession. For example, there are times when people will ask me to pray for a particular issue. Maybe the issue is insomnia. I will pray the Word – "He giveth His beloved sleep." The Holy Spirit will give me the revelation that I need to deal with the terror by night. Other times, He will tell me to rebuke the pestilence that walketh in darkness. When I pray by revelation, I get quicker results than when I pray using just my understanding of the Scriptures.

Keys stand for revelation and it enables you to know what to bind and loose in prayer. To have dominion on the Earth, you must have revelation of the ordinances of Heaven. You have to know what is bound in Heaven and what is loosed in Heaven so that you can walk in dominion:

Knowest thou the ordinances of heaven? canst thou set the dominion thereof in the earth. (Job 38:32)

Revelation enables you to know what Heaven has already determined concerning issues and matters of the Earth and this revelation gives you audacity to walk in dominion on the

Earth.

It is by prayer that we gain access to the Throne Room and the courts of Heaven to plead our case before the Father. Prayer must be executed so that what is written in the volume of the books concerning you, your family, your church, and your nation can be enforced.

The Bible tells us that we are to be gatekeepers. If we operate in the keys of revelation, which comes through intercessory prayers, it is then that the gates of Hell cannot prevail against us. It is when we understand this that we have power to bind and to loose and can enforce the Word.

It is the keys we receive in prayer by revelation that gives us the audacity to loose the manifestation of what has already been set in motion in Heaven and to bind the interference and the resistance from the enemy.

Wherefore we would have come unto you, even I Paul, once and again; but Satan hindered us. (1 Thessalonians 2:18)

Our prayers, even our revelatory prayers, must be consistent. Satan will hinder us in the Earth, but he will also attempt to block our prayers if we are not persistent in prayer.

But the prince of the kingdom of Persia withstood me one and twenty days: but, lo, Michael, one of the chief princes, came to help me; and I remained there with the kings of Persia. (Daniel 10:13)

This is how intercessors exercise their authority in prayer. Jesus told his disciples that when He left the Earth, He would ask the Father to send the Holy Spirit and give them access to the Father through prayer.

> *"And in that day ye shall ask me nothing. Verily, verily, I say unto you, Whatsoever ye shall ask the Father in my name, He will give it you." (John 16:23)*

Here we see that we have the authority of transfer. We are the gatekeepers and it is by prayer that we exercise this Divine Authority in the Name of Jesus.

What is prayer?

Prayer is a spiritual weapon that enables us to access the Kingdom of Heaven. *Prayer* is a guided missile. *Prayer* transcends boundaries and knows no limits. *Prayer* overrides the enemy and it exposes his agenda. It is in the place of prayer that the will of God is enforced and that His Kingdom is made manifest on earth and among men. That is why, in Luke 11:2, Jesus instructs us *pray* that "Thy Kingdom Come and let Thy will be done." He didn't say preach or sing that Thy Kingdom Come; he said **pray** *that Thy Kingdom Come.*

Chapter Summary:

- Prayer is our invitation from God to His Throne Room

- In the Beginning, before the Fall, there was no need for prayer. Man had Dominion.

- Prayer is a Tool and a Weapon

- Prayer is our opportunity to fellowship with God

- In order to be effective, prayers must be revelatory

- The keys to bind and loose are Keys to the Kingdom revealed in prayer

- It is the keys of revelation that help us be effective when dealing with Satan

- We must destroy the Kingdom of Satan and superimpose the Kingdom of God through revelatory Prayers.

- Prayers must be persistent in order to break the resistance of Satan.

Chapter 2

The Dominion Mandate

*"We must begin to believe that God, in the mystery of prayer, has entrusted us with a force that can move the Heavenly world, and can bring its power down to earth." – **Andrew Murray***

Regardless of how things may appear on the surface, nothing of eternal value is ever released without somebody, somewhere praying. God moves when His people pray.

In the beginning, there was no need for prayer. Man had unrestricted communion and fellowship with God. Man spoke and whatever he said was established. He named the animals and the woman with final authority. Whatever man needed, God knew beforehand and supplied even before man asked. He provided a garden, four rivers, substance for food and companionship. Man had dominion. This is called the Dominion Mandate:

Then God said, "Let us make man in our image, after our likeness. And let them have dominion over the fish of the sea and over the birds of the heavens and over the livestock and over all the earth and over every creeping thing that creeps on the earth.

So God created man in his own image, in the image of God he created him; male and female he created them. And God blessed them.

And God said to them, "Be fruitful and multiply and fill the earth and subdue it, and have dominion over the fish of the sea and over the birds of the heavens and over every living thing that moves on the earth." (Gen. 1:26-28)

God's original plan was for man to have dominion, rulership and governance over the affairs of the Earth. God created the man in the image of the Godhead and then blessed the man to rule the Earth. He did not place Himself in the position to rule the Earth, but gave man everything he would need to rule the domain of the Earth.

When Man ceded the Dominion Mandate to Satan through deception and high treason, God's agenda for man was interfered with. The woman by listening to the voice of Satan, was deceived by Satan.

1 Tim 2:13, says, "For Adam was formed first, then Eve; and Adam was not deceived, but the woman was deceived and became a transgressor."

Because the man did not overrule the deception, but permitted it to stand, Adam gave up his authority and handed over the Dominion of the Earth. Satan took over that governance and now controls the affairs of men. Satan knows he has this authority and he is willing to use it.

And the devil, taking him up into an high mountain, shewed unto him all the kingdoms of the world in a moment of time. And the devil said unto him, All this power will I give thee, and the glory of them: for that is delivered unto me; and to whomsoever I will I give it. (Luke 4:5-6)

When we ceded our Dominion Mandate, the lease Adam was

given on the Earth was handed over to Satan. The Bible says:

Therefore, rejoice, O heavens and you who dwell in them! But woe to you, O earth and sea, for the devil has come down to you in great wrath, because he knows that his time is short. (Revelation 12:12)

He is aware of the lease expiration and he is working with that in mind. His greatest weapon is keeping us blind and in darkness.

In whom the <u>god</u> of this world hath blinded the minds of them which believe not, lest the light of the glorious gospel of Christ, who is the image of <u>God</u>, should shine unto them. (2 Corinthians 4:4)

The first "god" in this scripture is lower case. This is in reference to Satan. The second God, is God the Father. So it is Satan that has blinded the minds of others, but God the Father, desires that we walk in illumination. When people ask why a loving God allows bad things to happen in this world, we should be mindful that Satan is the god of this world. If we want our Father to come onto the scene, Jesus states we have to pray **"Thy Kingdom Come and thy will be done on Earth as it is in Heaven." (Matthew 6:10)**

When God gave man the Dominion Mandate He did not say He would rule with us; it says "let us make man in our image.... and let them have dominion." Without an intercessor, God does not get involved in the affairs of men. It would violate the order He set in motion by giving Adam dominion.

If we say that God will get involved, but He does not get involved, we imply that He exercises His will and shows preference in what He personally prevents on Earth. Instead the Bible says:

Surely the Lord God will do nothing, but he revealeth his secret unto his servants the prophets. (Amos 3:3)

Everything God does and anything that happens in the Earth, He will reveal to a man in the Earth. That man has the assignment to intercede.

And I sought for a man among them, that should make up the hedge, and stand in the gap before me for the land, that I should not destroy it: but I found none. (Ezekiel 22:30)

Since the fall, everything God gets involved with requires prayer from men and women. Before that, Adam had fellowship and that fellowship produced a continual supply of whatever was required. Even unto today, the Lord Jesus Christ ever lives to intercede for us:

Wherefore he is able also to save them to the uttermost that come unto God by him, seeing he ever liveth to make intercession for them. (Hebrews 7:25)

Indeed, when we pray the Holy Spirit gives us revelation as we pray to help direct and guide us through our own personal time of prayer:

Likewise the Spirit also helpeth our infirmities: for we know not what we should pray for as we ought: but the Spirit itself maketh intercession for us with groanings which cannot be uttered. And he that searcheth the hearts knoweth what is the mind of the Spirit, because he maketh intercession for the saints according to the will of God. (Romans 8:26-27)

Christ came as a man -- not a spirit-- to redeem us and to

restore the first dominion. The first Adam was justified by the second (Jesus Christ).

> *For if by one man's offence death reigned by one; much more they which receive abundance of grace and of the gift of righteousness shall reign in life by one, Jesus Christ. (Romans 5:17)*

If we say that God "will not" - it implies that He *can* intervene but chooses *not to intervene* in the affairs of men. It also –suggests that He is in charge of the Earth and that the calamities of the Earth could be prevented if only God chose to prevent them.

While it is true that there are rules of engagement that the universe itself deploys in defense of the Earth, God has given man dominion over the Earth and He -- God -- does not have that dominion. We are warned of dangers in the realm of intercession and we have a responsibility to stand in the gap and lift up prayer.

> *"And I sought for a man among them, that should make up the hedge, and stand in the gap before me for the land, that I should not destroy it: but I found none." (Ezekiel 22:30)*

So when people --believers and unbelievers -- ask, "Why does a good God let bad things happen?" we must acknowledge that not everything that happens is orchestrated or can be prevented by God. Satan is the god of this world. He is behind and orchestrates the calamities and disasters. Some things are programmed as a result of iniquity and sin. It takes prayers and intercession to avert danger and calamity. God will help us, but He has put the responsibility on us to pray and ask Him to get involved. Romans 8 says that all of creation, which is affected by the fall, is looking for man to take their rightful place and discover their adoption as sons of God.

If we say that God will intervene without prayer, it is not scripturally correct. That would negate the necessity for prayers, a watchman, intercession and the Spirit of Prophecy, which is Jesus Christ coming to redeem and restore us to the first dominion.

The earth was not created for God to rule - it was created for men to have rulership – dominion. This is why we have binding and loosing authority in prayer to destroy Satan's rulership and to negate his ability to hinder us and keep us from enforcing the Kingdom of God in the Earth.

We have to say, as uncomfortable as it is, that when we do not invite God to be a part of the solution through our prayers, God is not obligated to intervene. It is not because He will not, but because we have not asked Him to get involved and it is our responsibility to engage God in the affairs of the governance of the Earth. There are things that God cannot do and He set it up that way. He cannot lie; He cannot worship Himself. He cannot fail. He also cannot violate the will of man because HE gave man free will to use for or against Him because He didn't create man as robots.
In the Garden of Eden the reason why Adam and Eve were able to sin is because God gave them free will. The absence of free will violates the very essence of God's nature, which

is love. Love does not force itself upon man --- violating his will. The difference between the first and the second Adam (Jesus) is that the first Adam exercised his will against God; the second Adam (Jesus) submitted His will to God. He has made Himself subject to His Word and placed certain responsibilities in the hands of men through Christ who is our chief Intercessor. God needs an intercessor to stand in the gap – even Christ who lives forever to intercede for us and who has ordained us to a royal priesthood, a holy nation after the order of Melchizedek so that we can intercede for others in prayer.

It is by prayer that we communicate with God to bring the heavenly decrees, revelatory purposes and written judgments of the Kingdom of God into the Earth realm and override the power of the Kingdom of Satan.

Until Adam's lease expires, Satan still rules over the affairs of men and that is the main reason why prayer is a daily necessity for daily triumph. We cannot cease praying. It is our job to pray, it is Satan's job to resist our prayers. Satan puts up a resistance when we pray, but we must remain vigilant. The Bible says –

Thou hast covered thyself with a cloud, that our prayer should not pass through. (Lamentations 3:44)

For we wrestle not against flesh and blood, but against principalities, against powers, against the rulers of the darkness of this world, against spiritual wickedness in high places. (Ephesians 6:12)

As long as Satan has the lease that Adam ceded to him,

prayer is the necessary tool to enforce God's original intent and bring the Kingdom of God on the scene in the affairs of men. It is in prayer that we exercise not only our dominion over the Earth but we take authority in the Heavens and over the interference of the enemy who is the prince of the power of the air – the blinding veil that blocks our heavens.

"And he will destroy in this mountain the face of the covering cast over all people, and the vail that is spread over all nations." (Isaiah 25:7)

This veil blocks us from receiving revelation from the realm of Heaven to keep us in the dark so that we never know what is happening behind the scenes. The veil keeps you ignorant so that you blame God for what is going on and you fail to recognize the schemes of the enemy that is operating to wreak havoc and destruction. Once the veil is lifted by illumination through prayer you are empowered to overrule the works of the enemy.

"Lest Satan should get an advantage of us: for we are not ignorant of his devices." (2 Corinthians 2:11)

The main purpose for the veil is to keep us blinded in the dark, ignorant, desensitized and eventually to discredit the Word of God to the believer so that we stop believing God's Word and we blame God for everything bad that happens to us. Because God sees all things and He is all knowing, we expect that He should prevent bad things from happening to us. But, God gave man dominion over the earth and the rules of engagement require that we pray, intercede and use the

Word of God to overrule, override and overturn the works of darkness. By discrediting the Word of God, he gets us to deny our faith and lose our hope in God's ability to help us. That is what Satan did to Adam and Eve in the Garden. He discredited the Word of God – which is our source and our weapon to destroy the veil and to keep him from operating behind the scenes. We use the Word to expose the works of darkness.

> *"For we wrestle not against flesh and blood, but against principalities, against powers, against the rulers of the darkness of this world, against spiritual wickedness in high places." (Ephesians 6:12)*

> *"(For the weapons of our warfare are not carnal, but mighty through God to the pulling down of strong holds;) Casting down imaginations, and every high thing that exalteth itself against the knowledge of God, and bringing into captivity every thought to the obedience of Christ; And having in a readiness to revenge all disobedience, when your obedience is fulfilled." (2 Cor. 10:4-6)*

These scriptures reveal that we are in an ongoing war with the unseen forces of darkness – persons without bodies. Our warfare is not with flesh and blood, but with disembodied spirits and the powers of darkness. We must not be afraid to confront them because you can never conquer what you are not willing to confront.

> *"And they overcame him by the blood of the Lamb, and by the word of their testimony; and they loved not their lives unto the death." (Rev. 12:11)*

Satan has power to control and manipulate the events that

happen in the Earth from his seat of power. He is a prince in his kingdom. Later we will discuss the hierarchy of Satan's kingdom. But, you must understand Satan has a kingdom.

Satan's kingdom mandate is to be a cloud of confusion that hinders the original plan of God and prevents the Kingdom of God from being made manifest. That's why Jesus said in Luke 11:2 for us to pray "Thy Kingdom Come" – not teach, but pray.

Intercessors are the most powerful people on the Earth today. Intercessors are appointed for the purpose of bringing God into the affairs of men. God will not intervene, unless someone prays.

It is only the Church in the Earth that has this authority. Scripture reveals that when Heaven is made manifest in the Earth, it is because of the *saints*. Our prayers have power to produce results on Earth. In the book of Revelation it says,

And another angel came and stood at the altar, having a golden censer; and there was given unto him much incense, that he should offer it with the <u>prayers of all saints</u> upon the golden altar which was before the throne. And the smoke of the incense, which came with <u>the prayers of the saints</u>, ascended up before God out of the angel's hand. And the angel took the censer, and filled it with fire of the altar, and cast it into the earth: and there were voices, and thunderings, and lightnings, and an earthquake. (Rev. 8:3-5)

It is the prayers of the saints that make the Heavens open and produce a response from our Father. When Jesus was baptized, He also came praying and the Heavens were opened.

Now when all the people were baptized, it came to pass, that Jesus also being baptized, and praying, the heaven was opened, And the Holy Ghost descended in a bodily shape like a dove upon him, and a voice came from heaven, which said, Thou art my beloved Son; in thee I am well pleased. (Luke 3:21-22)

We lost the first Dominion through the sin of independence from God. Before that, there was no need for prayer as we had continual fellowship with God. It is in the place of prayer that we regain and superimpose the first Dominion over the enemy.

When we ceded the Dominion Mandate to Satan, we came under the law of sin and death. But, when Christ died, He defeated death and removed the stain of sin so that the saints now have access to the Throne Room of Heaven. It is the Church alone in the Earth that has this power and mandate. Under Christ we are no more under the law of sin and death.

For the law of the Spirit of life in Christ Jesus hath made me free from the law of sin and death. (Romans 8:2)

Jesus defeated Death. Death is the entry gate to the kingdom of Satan. No one enters Hell until they pass through Death. It is through prayer that we destroy the kingdom of Darkness and enforce the judgment written that the Gates of Hell shall not prevail against us. Jesus told us to pray Thy kingdom come so that we can destroy the kingdom of Satan and make the kingdoms of this world the kingdom of our God and His Christ. God's Kingdom is His governmental authority.

How do the kingdoms of this world become the Kingdoms of our God and His Christ? By superimposing God's governmental authority and His rule over the kingdoms of this world through relentless prayer.

In **Luke 18:1, Jesus says** *"….. men ought always to pray, and not to faint."* We must not get weary in prayer. We must keep praying until our prayers are answered.

Isaiah 62:6-7 says *"I have set watchmen upon thy walls, O Jerusalem, which shall never hold their peace day nor night: ye that make mention of the Lord keep not silence, And give him no rest, till he establish, and till he make Jerusalem a praise in the earth."* We cannot hold our peace and sit by idle and wondering what will happen. God wants us to "give Him no rest" until our prayers are answered.

1 Thessalonians 5:17 tells us to, *"pray without ceasing."* It is persistent prayer that breaks resistance. *Prayer is a daily necessity for daily triumph.*

God has chosen to govern His Kingdom by the simple law of asking and receiving. It is the anointed strategy of God. Jesus told us:

Ask and it will be given to you; seek and you will find; knock and the door will be opened to you. For everyone who asks receives. (Matt. 7:7-8)

God said to the Prophet Jeremiah:

Call unto me, and I will answer thee, and show thee great and mighty things, which thou knowest not. (Jeremiah 33: 3)

Paul the Apostle wrote:

> ***Blessed be the God and Father of our Lord Jesus Christ, who has blessed us with every spiritual blessing in the heavenly places in Christ. (Ephesians 1:3)***

If the blessings of God are in the heavenly realms, how do we bring them down?

The Church has to open up Heaven and summon the power of God. We have to petition Him for Heaven to react to what we pray. We pray according to His Word. Throughout God's Word we see that supernatural acts are available from a supernatural God to a certain kind of people. To people who will love Him, God is willing to give unlimited favor and miracles. The Bible says over and over that He keeps covenant with those who love Him and keep His commandments. Prayer gives those who love Him the power to enforce His commandments.

God exercises His authority and ability to do the impossible through the prayers of His people. Our level of influence is limited until we enter into prayer – direct fellowship, intimacy and communion between a Holy God and a regenerated, spirit-filled vessel produces tremendous impact and the necessary force to change situations.

Those who have not received the Gospel message of Jesus Christ will never be brought into the Kingdom without the spirit led prayers of someone. Jesus says:

> ***Therefore said he unto them, The harvest truly is great, but the***

labourers are few: pray ye therefore the Lord of the harvest, that he would send forth labourers into his harvest. (Luke 10:2)

Paul tells us it is a continual process and we must travail for others:

My little children, of whom I travail in birth again until Christ be formed in you. (Galatians 4:19)

The reason people stop praying is because of the reactions of the enemy. The reactions are a result of your prayers. The enemy will intimidate you to cause you to doubt your prayers are working in order to make you stop praying. All the while, he will continue to fight and harass you. He will intimidate you by force to convince you that your prayers are the cause of new issues and you are doing something wrong. The threats and intimidation are designed to de-sensitize and deceive you and to make you believe that your prayers are not working so you will stop praying. But, don't stop! The reactions are an indication that your prayers *are* working. Your persistence will break the resistance. The Bible says:

And let us not be weary in well doing: for in due season we shall reap, if we faint not. (Galatians 6:9)

You have to keep speaking the Word to activate, engage and deploy angelic assistance. Scriptures say in **Hebrews 1:14 "Are they not all ministering spirits, <u>sent forth to minister for them</u> who shall be heirs of salvation?"** They work for the heirs of salvation. The angels move at the command of His Word executed in prayer. The Bible says:

Bless the Lord, ye his angels, that excel in strength, that do his

> *commandments, hearkening unto the VOICE of his word. (Psalm 103:20)*

The enemy will not release those held captive unless he is bound and his diabolical opposition against the Kingdom of God is destroyed. It is through prayer that the prison doors are opened. It is a tragic loss to the Kingdom of God for a Christian to say that he loves the souls of men, but fails to passionately pray for them.

The Church prayed for Peter and an Angel was released. The Bible says –

> *Peter therefore was kept in prison: but prayer was made without ceasing of the church unto God for him. (Acts 12:5)*

The enemy will not just release captives because we confess scriptures. We must pray without ceasing to deploy angelic assistance.

> *And, behold, the angel of the Lord came upon him, and a light shined in the prison: and he smote Peter on the side, and raised him up, saying, Arise up quickly. And his chains fell off from his hands. And the angel said unto him, Gird thyself, and bind on thy sandals. And so he did. And he saith unto him, Cast thy garment about thee, and follow me. (Acts 12:7-8)*

If we will pray with force, God will do miraculous things that exceed our imagination.

> *Now unto Him that is able to do exceeding abundantly above all that we ask or think, according to the power that worketh in us. (Ephesians 3:20)*

Our prayers are an indication of the power at work in us. Paul and Silas prayed at midnight – a key time for intercession – and their prayers were answered in a way no one could have imagined:

> *And at midnight Paul and Silas prayed, <u>and sang praises unto God</u>: and the prisoners heard them. And suddenly there was a great earthquake, so that the foundations of the prison were shaken: and immediately all the doors were opened, and every one's bands were loosed. (Acts 16:25-26)*

A prayerless Christian and a prayerless church will never be able to exercise the Dominion Mandate. The answer is according to the power at work in you. If you want more power when dealing with the enemy, you must spend time in prayer. Prayer moves God!

Prayer binds the enemy and opens the heavens. It is the plow that breaks up the fallow ground for the Gospel seed and ushers in the manifest glory of the Kingdom of Jesus Christ. Prayer is one of God's primary means of Grace to achieve the desires of His heart. Thus, it is not an exaggeration to say that the most powerful person on the earth is one that knows how to pray.

> *The earnest (heartfelt, continued) prayer of a righteous man makes tremendous power available [dynamic in its working]. (James 5:16)*

This means that effectual fervent prayer makes tremendous power available to the people of God.

Chapter Summary:

- In the Beginning, before the Fall, there was no need for prayer. Man had Dominion. This is called the Dominion Mandate.

- God's original plan was for man to have dominion over the affairs of the Earth.

- The woman, being deceived by Satan transgressed by doubting what God had already revealed. The man did not overrule the deception and ceded the dominion of the Earth to Satan through this act of high treason.

- The lease Adam was given on the Earth now is in the hands of Satan and Satan uses our ignorance of God's ordinances to govern the affairs of the Earth.

- Satan is the god of this world. He uses his position to blind us. He understands it is by prayer that we can overrule his kingdom and enforce the Kingdom of God.

- God gets involved in the affairs of the Earth, when a man or woman invites Him through prayers.

- Our major weapon against Satan is prayer. Especially revelatory prayers. Persistent and consistent prayers. Persistence will break his resistance.

- Satan's major weapon to keep us ignorant is to keep us in darkness and blind using a veil of sin and spiritual resistance to keep our prayers from being effective

- Christ intercedes for us. The Holy Spirit intercedes for us. But, always God is looking for and will speak through intercessors to pray Thy Kingdom come, Thy Will be done in Earth as it is in Heaven.

- We must invite God through intercession to be a part of the solution to the issues and problems we face on Earth

- Satan's kingdom is ruled by unseen forces and persons without bodies. Their weapon is a blinding veil that covers us until we persist in prayer, destroy the veil and break the resistance.

- Persistent prayer, intercession – is warfare prayer. We wrestle not against flesh and blood, but we do wrestle against spiritual wickedness in high places.

- This kind of prayer will cause you to work up a sweat. But, it will also cause you to walk in tremendous power – dynamic in its working.

- The power to enforce the Dominion Mandate is available to us, the Church in this dispensation. We exercise our dominion through prayer.

Chapter 3

Revival Fires

Oh! men and brethren, what would this heart feel if I could but believe that there were some among you who would go home and pray for a revival - men whose faith is large enough, and their love fiery enough to lead them from this moment to exercise unceasing intercessions that God would appear among us and do wondrous things here, as in the times of former generations. – **C.H. Spurgeon**

Throughout history and even now there are men and women of renown who prayed for nations, kings and leaders, whose prayers have shown to produce tremendous breakthroughs in the Earth and in the Heavens. The Bible says in Isaiah 64:1 –

Oh that thou wouldest rend the heavens, that thou wouldest come down, that the mountains might flow down at thy presence.

Revival doesn't just happen. Reformation doesn't just happen. Regeneration is not a product of confession alone. It is in the furnace of travailing prayers that these golden treasures of our life in Christ are solidly forged. If we forsake prayer, even scheduled events that God intends to shape the destiny of nations can be lost.

Revival is when God gets so sick and tired of being misrepresented that He shows Himself. – **Leonard Ravenhill**

I always say, "True Revival is when God comes to town." Throughout this book we will examine prayer and reveal how we have a responsibility to pray and bring God on the scene in the affairs of men. When we do this, we will see revivals greater than we have ever seen before in the lives of men, women, families, churches, nations and our world. Ordinary men and women like D. L. Moody, Smith Wigglesworth, Charles Finney, A. A. Allen, John G. Lake, Maria Woodworth- Etter, Kathryn Kuhlman, John Alexander Dowie and others, prayed and God came to town. The common theme in their diverse ministries and the age and time that God used them was their dedication to prayer and praying for the Kingdom of God and the Holy Spirit to come in power. It wasn't just their fiery oratory, but they prayed with great passion and by the revelation of the Holy Spirit. It was their intercession that released the manifestation of great spiritual awakening and times of revival, restoration and reformation. Throughout their ministries, there were prophecies and testimonies of revival fires that would usher in the move of God and ultimately that will precede the coming of the Lord Jesus Christ. I want to use this chapter to show you some times of prayer that we are benefitting from today and to let you know there are prophecies that we will see a great revival in the Earth in the years ahead like never before. But, Beloved, every prophecy is conditional. It is not automatic. In Ezekiel 36, God makes many promises to Israel. Over and over again, He says what He will do for the Israelites and how He will bless and deliver them. But, after all His promises, in verse 37 He says:

> *"Thus saith the Lord God; I will yet for this be enquired of by the house of Israel, to do it for them..."*

In 1 Kings 18, Elijah, an ordinary man like you and I, had the ability to travail in prayer and execute the judgment written and his prayers shut the heavens due to the disobedience of the nation. James 5 shows us he had to travail again in prayer to enforce the prophecy and release the rain.

In 1 Timothy 1:18, Paul admonishes "This charge I commit unto thee, son Timothy, according to the prophecies which went before on thee, that thou by them mightest war a good warfare." You must war to secure your prophetic destiny!

Just because it belongs to you, doesn't mean you can have it. There's a great revival that belongs to this generation, but if we are going to see it – we will need to intercede and get serious with God in times of dedicated prayer.

The Bible says, "And from the days of John the Baptist until now the kingdom of heaven suffereth violence, and the violent take it by force" (Matthew 11:12). You must be willing to go to war in prayer and vigorously contend with the Word over your life, your children, your marriage, your church, your city and your nation.

If revival depended on you -- your prayers, your faith, your obedience -- would your church ever experience revival? – **Del Fehsenfeld Jr.**

When the Apostle Paul said he labored in prayer –

> **"Whereunto I labor also, striving according to His working which worketh in me mightily." (Colossians 1:29)**

The Apostle is using the same word for labor ward – to travail as a woman does in birth. Prayers to bring others into the Kingdom is a serious matter –

> *"Epaphras, who is one of you, a servant of Christ, saluteth you, always labouring fervently for you in prayers, that ye may stand perfect and complete in all the will of God." (Col. 4:12)*

If we are going to see the great revival that is scheduled for this age, we must be willing to labor in prayer. I want you to read these historic accounts with that in mind. Be encouraged that no matter what, you will seek to walk away from reading this book fully energized and committed to praying for the greatest revival this earth has ever seen.

> *"Wherefore we would have come unto you, even I Paul, once and again; but Satan hindered us." (I Thessalonians 1:18)*

The enemy will resist you. Satan will try to stop you. Wickedness will oppose the cause of the righteous, but you are destined for greatness and if you persist in prayer, you will break every resistance of the enemy. Your persistent, effective prayer has great power to change the course of destiny and make an impact in the lives of generations yet unborn.

The difference between ordinary men and those who change the course of destinies and lives is their willingness to lay aside their own agenda and to risk their own personal preservation to ensure the destinies of nations and to enforce the agenda of the Lord Jesus Christ in their day and time. If we are going to be relevant in this age and the age to come, we must be willing to labor in prayer to override the agenda of the enemy and to superimpose God's agenda over the enemy's agenda.

Bold men fearlessly bring change wherever they find themselves on the Earth. They don't let captivity restrict them or their circumstances hinder their ability to engage the Hand of Elohim to intervene in the affairs of men. They understand that the mortality of the flesh is no match for the immortality of effectual, fervent intercessory prayers.

And they overcame him by the blood of the Lamb, and by the word of their testimony; and they loved not their lives unto the death. (Revelation 12:11)

John Knox

John Knox was considered one of the most powerful preachers of his day. He was a Scottish clergyman, a writer and a leader of the Protestant Reformation. He is considered the founder of the Presbyterian denomination in Scotland. In a relentless campaign of fiery oratory, he sought to destroy idolatry and to purify Scotland's religion.

Knox was taken prisoner by French forces in 1547 and exiled to England upon his release in 1549. While in exile, he was licensed to work in the Church of England, where he rose in the ranks to serve King Edward VI of England as a royal chaplain. He exerted a reforming influence on the text of the *Book of Common Prayer.* He was influential in the courts of kings, but he was most influential in the courts of Elohim.

In one of his most famous political battles, as he stood on the front lines as a watchman to enforce The Protestant Reformation, he opposed Mary Queen of Scots. She would call on Knox to change his position on her personal rulership and he stood before her and maintained his convictions. When Mary asked him whether subjects had a right, according to the Bible, to resist their ruler, he replied that if monarchs exceeded their lawful limits, they might be resisted, even by force.

When she tried to get him to alter his sermons to reflect her in a better light or at least to run his messages by her first, he told her he would not wait for her permission. At one point Catholic priests defied the laws set in motion by Reformation related to taking Catholic Mass and members of the Reformation publicly opposed the Catholic priests. Mary chose this occasion to summon Knox again to make the reformers back down. Instead, by the end of their meeting, Mary agreed to have the Catholic priests arrested for breaking the laws of the Reformation.

When she wanted to marry Don Carlos of Spain, a Catholic, Knox openly opposed the union. Mary summoned him yet again and began to cry in his presence. He basically told her that her tears were not enough to make him "betray the Commonwealth."

Knox was bold in addressing the nation and leadership, preaching fiery messages calling for repentance. In response to Knox's imprecatory prayers, Mary Queen of Scots is reputed to have said, "I fear the prayers of John Knox more than all the assembled armies of Europe."

John Knox saw how important it was for the church to do what the Bible said, and not just what it thought was right. He wasn't afraid to stand up to anyone for what he knew was right. His preaching and prayers were used by God to transform the whole of Scotland and when he was buried, it was said that 'Here lies a man who in his life never feared the face of man."

John Knox prayed and exercised the Dominion Mandate against the seat of power in his day. He did not let Mary Queen of Scots or any power operating behind the scenes overrule the Word of God he gained through prayer and staying committed to his mission. If we are going to see governmental reformation and truly bring the Kingdom of God to the kingdoms of this world, we will need to be like John Knox and exercise the Dominion Mandate only available in times of prayer and intercession.

John Knox prayed for the Kingdom of God to come:

But, O Lord, infinite in mercy ... let thy kingdom shortly come, that sin may be ended, death devoured, thy enemies confounded; that we thy people, by thy majesty delivered, may obtain everlasting joy and felicity, through Jesus Christ our Saviour, to whom be all honour and praise, forever. Amen.

Evan John Roberts

The whole world felt the impact of revival that swept Wales from November 1904 through 1905, with mainly young people engaged in intense prayers of intercession and a "new move" of the infilling of the Holy Spirit.

Evan John Roberts began studying for the ministry at Newcastle Emlyn in 1904. He received the Baptism of the Holy Spirit at a service held by Evangelist Seth Joshua in Cardigan. He was invigorated to pray and began to preach in small meetings. His intense prayers and four-point sermons started attracting very large crowds in the thousands and put him at the helm of one of the greatest revivals of our time, the Welsh Revival.

The four points of his message were:

1. Confess all known sin and give up every vice.
2. Remove anything in your life that you are in doubt or feel unsure about. Even if you don't know if it is good or bad, give it up anyway. Be ready to remove any cloud that blocks your ability to access Heaven.
3. Be ready to obey the Holy Spirit instantly. Whatever He says, just do it.
4. Publicly confess the Lord Jesus Christ.

Of his early years, he later wrote, "I said to myself: I will have the Spirit . . . for ten or eleven years I have prayed for revival. I could sit up all night to read or talk about revivals. It was the Spirit who moved me to think about revival." One night he had a supernatural encounter during prayer where he reported being "taken up in Glory." He was so overcome that the bed he was lying in began to shake and woke his brother, who took him for ill.

Every night for three months, Roberts would be awakened by the Holy Spirit at 1:00 a.m. to be "taken up into divine fellowship" and would proceed to pray until 5:00 a.m. He would then fall back to sleep for four hours before waking again at 9:00 a.m. and continuing in prayer until noon. During this time he received a burden for the Revival of Wales. He spent hours just praying for souls.

One day in prayer, he had a vision of young men from his town asking him to come and pray for them. He tried to shake the vision out of his head, but it wouldn't go away. He said "Lord, if it is Your will, I will go." He left immediately for his hometown. Within two weeks, he was leading meetings in his hometown and thousands were being saved weekly until, within a year, more than 100,000 had come to the Lord in his meetings.

The theme of the Welsh Revivals was a call to repentance and waiting for the Holy Spirit to move. People came in masses to meeting halls from everywhere, confessing and experiencing the conviction of sin. In the presence of the Holy Spirit, people from all walks of life spoke of wanting to give up their vices. Some gave up liquor and places of ill repute. Some gave up football (Rugby as it is called in that part of the country) – one of the most popular sports in all of Wales – not because it was bad itself, according to a London pastor, but because players and fans were prone to drink and gamble during the games.

Given that one of Roberts' four points was that believers should give up anything they were unsure about, the football fans determined that the temptations were not worth risking their standing with God. Their love for football was replaced by a zeal for God. Women whose husbands had refused to go to church were now meeting them in the sanctuary, having forsaken stadiums of sports for prayer meetings.

There were thousands of conversions that brought tremendous joy. Some of the toughest characters in the Welsh valleys were converted. It was a revival that was begun and sustained especially by the young.

Roberts' meetings were opened by worship in song and he often would agonize for hours waiting for The Holy Spirit before bringing any message. Sometimes he didn't preach at all, he just let the "Holy Spirit have His way." The services would often last for many hours and run through the night into the early hours. He would close the services and still wake early to pray and invite men who worked in the coalmines to the meetings.

Roberts was disciplined in his prayer life and prayer was his main ministry.

Later in his life, he took refuge to pray in England and wouldn't return to Wales even upon invitation. His desire to pray for souls and abandon what he considered to be theatrics related to the revival (someone once showed up at a meeting to hypnotize him) made him dedicate more time to pray than to speak publicly. He believed he could do more to win souls in prayer than he could in the meetings preaching to thousands. He became convinced that the work of intercession was vital to win souls. There are several accounts of how he continued the mission on his knees and with his writings, encouraging the missionary growth of the 20th century.

Evan Roberts in his later years would pray mostly in private, interceding for Christian leaders and believers around the world. Evan Roberts exercised the Dominion Mandate in prayer knowing that his battle was not with flesh and blood, but spiritual wickedness in high places. He was willing until the end of his life to fight and labor in prayer. He was persistent and consistent because he realized that it was only this kind of constant prayer that would be able to break the resistance of the enemy. He spoke of the special circumstances of the strategic warfare of a committed prayer life:

In Luke, it does not say, "preach and faint not," but "*pray* and faint not." It is not difficult to preach. But while you pray, you are alone in some solitary place, fighting in a prayer-battle against the powers of darkness. And you will know the secret of victory.

William Seymour

William Seymour was born in Centerville, Louisiana in 1870 to former slaves. He grew up in extreme poverty and during a time of racial injustice and violence towards African-Americans. In his youth, Seymour taught himself to read by using the Bible. It was during this time that his hunger grew for the Word of God and that he knew his freedom would come from Jesus Christ. He suffered so much racial injustice in the South that he believed the true revival would come as the races fellowshipped together. This was such a foreign notion at that time that even people like Charles Parham, a major influence on the early movement of Pentecostalism, and an initial mentor and benefactor to Seymour, ended up dividing with him on his commitment to violate the separatism that existed in the churches during his early ministry. Charles Parham believed the churches should remain segregated.

In the 1890s, Seymour left the South in order to travel north. He joined a number of churches and eventually was called to ministry in 1895. Prior to accepting his call, he became sick with small pox and lost his sight in one eye. This handicap and his adherence to the "Holiness movement" of that day; drove him to attach his condition to God's "punishment" for not accepting his call earlier. It was this incident that lead him to pray with seriousness and single-minded vision. He was known to sometimes even put a cardboard box over his head to be completely focused on prayer and waiting for the move of the Holy Spirit during services and times of preaching and teaching God's Word. As strange as his behavior was, it was this single-minded devotion that birthed a movement that is still celebrated all over the world.

During Seymour's travels, he was greatly influenced by the Holiness movement and additionally by groups that were dedicated to racial equality. The idea of a racially desegregated church influenced his theology and was a great part of the Azusa Street Revival and the various ministries that were birthed during that time. In fact, along with a host of other controversies that surrounded the Revival, his use of white itinerant evangelists became a point of contention from the blacks that served in the work at Azusa Street.

Shortly before the Azusa Street Revival, Seymour became acquainted with Charles Parham in Houston, Texas. In fact, it was Charles Parham who provided him with the finances and sent him as a missionary to California. Charles Parham is one of the early founders of the Assemblies of God churches. At the time, Parham wanted to minister to the whites and wanted Seymour to minister to the blacks. Because of this many believed Parham to be racist, but Parham was a product of the times of racial segregation in the South. It was Parham's teachings on the baptism of the Holy Spirit that moved Seymour and convinced him it was his duty to pray for the infilling of the Holy Spirit. Seymour and Parham differed on a number of doctrinal issues and eventually separated because of scandal surrounding Parham's ministry.

Seymour believed in glossolalia ("speaking in tongues") as a confirmation of the infilling of the Holy Spirit when he witnessed it from one of his followers. He believed in the "holiness" doctrine that was popular at that time – and that is still somewhat popular today – that you cannot go to Heaven unless you have demonstrated the infilling of the Holy Spirit with the outward manifestation of speaking in tongues. During this Revival, there was such a global outbreak and diversity of gifts that it became characteristic of doctrinal divisions and this was certainly a major one that kept him from being accepted in many circles until after his death.

When Seymour got to Los Angeles, he encountered very interesting trials that birthed a time of intensely passionate prayers that preceded the beginning of the Azusa Street Revival. He attended a meeting where Evan Roberts came fresh from the Welsh Revival and he heard stories of people being baptized in "the Holy Spirit", which solidified his belief that he should press for this gift in prayer. He studied the scriptures and started a Bible Study using it as a topic at the mission house he had been invited to stay as a guest. As a result, the owners of the mission house locked him out for being a heretic. He went to stay at the house of a couple who attended his Bible Study at the mission and locked himself in his room and spent intense times wrestling in prayer. The couple soon started hosting a prayer meeting in their home. Seymour encouraged everyone to embark on a 10-day fast for the infilling of the Holy Spirit. During this period, a member of the prayer group became ill. Seymour laid hands on the man and he was instantly healed and began to speak in tongues. At the next Bible Study, as they gave testimony others were healed and also began to speak in tongues. At this point, Seymour himself still did not have the evidence. He prayed more earnestly for this supernatural gift of glossolalia. Three days later, the house where the prayer meetings were being held was filled with people being healed and being baptized in the Holy Ghost. Three days after the initial person was filled, Seymour received the infilling of the Holy Spirit with the evidence of speaking in tongues.

The Miracle of Azusa Street has had a resounding effect on the Church even unto today. The Movement spread around the world under the exciting ministries of the Azusa Street Pilgrims who received their Pentecostal experiences at Azusa Street. Among them were G.B. Cashwell (the American South), C.H. Mason (The Church of God in Christ), William H. Durham (Chicago, the American Midwest, and Canada), Mary Rumsey (Korea), A.H. Argue (Canada), and John G. Lake (South Africa). Later, those indirectly influenced by Azusa Street took the Pentecostal message and experience around the world. These included Thomas Ball Barratt (Western Europe and Great Britain), Daniel Berg and Gunnar Vingren (Brazil), Luigi Francescon (Italy, Argentina, and Brazil), and Ivan Voronaev (Russia and the Slavic nations).

Azusa Street influenced the reformation and stabilization of the Church of God in Christ (Memphis, Tennessee), the Pentecostal Holiness Church (North Carolina), The Church of God (Cleveland, Tennessee), the United Holy Church (North Carolina), and the Pentecostal Free Will Baptist Church (North Carolina). Additionally, this Pentecostal movement marked by the outpouring of the Holy Spirit birthed churches like the Assemblies of God (Missouri), the Pentecostal Church of God (Missouri), the International

Church of the Foursquare Gospel (California), as well as the Oneness denominations: the Pentecostal Assemblies of the World (Indiana), and the United Pentecostal Church (Missouri). Every classical Pentecostal movement around the world can trace its spiritual roots, directly or indirectly, to the humble mission on Azusa Street. Beloved, one man, locked in a room, single-mindedly focused on God and a prophetic word that had been hanging in the balance for decades – brought about a move that is still reverberating in the earth today. This is the Dominion Mandate in action.

After only one century, the Pentecostal movement birthed in Azusa, California has grown to be second in size only to the Roman Catholic Church as a worldwide family of churches. This is the activity of what happens when God comes to town.

The amazing thing about this Pentecostal movement that gripped the world in 1906 and didn't seem to settle down until around 1915 – is that there was a prophecy given by the two fathers of the revival. The prophecy was given while the two men were at odds with one another and from two different places almost simultaneously. It is recorded that Seymour and Parham both prophesied in late 1909, on the same day – Seymour from Los Angeles and Parham in Houston – they both prophesied the Azusa glory, the shekinah glory, would return to earth after 100 years from the end of the Revival – not just in Azusa, but now it would be everywhere. Even more amazing is one of the founders of the Welsh Revival; Smith Wigglesworth confirmed the prophecy at the end of his life in 1939. It is recorded that in 1939 Smith Wigglesworth prophesied to Lester Sumrall about the final wave of God's glory. Lester Sumrall recorded that Smith Wigglesworth said:

"After that, after the third wave," he started sobbing. "I see the last day revival that's going to usher in the precious fruit of the earth. It will be the greatest revival this world has ever seen! It's going to be a wave of the gifts of the Spirit. The ministry gifts will be flowing on this planet earth. I see hospitals being emptied out, and they will bring the sick to churches where they allow the Holy Ghost to move." – Smith Wigglesworth on Latter Rain Revival

We are in a season where if we are willing to exercise our Dominion Mandate and labor in travailing prayers for God to come to town, we can war with the prophecy of these great revivalists to see a end-time revival that will sweep the globe with the charismatic gifts of the Spirit and the Lord will be present to heal. Let us never grow weary as we seek the Lord for this word to be fulfilled in our lifetime!

John Hyde

John Hyde was the son of a Presbyterian minister. He was called to the mission field and in 1892 he went to India with the great hope of evangelizing the Punjabi. On the way, he read a letter from a friend who said he would pray for John to be filled with the Holy Spirit to empower him to pray. John, offended, threw the letter away. Little did he know, he would need the power of the Holy Spirit for the work set before him.

Hyde's inability to master the complex native languages in India, and the fact that he was facing millions of unsaved natives with only five missionaries; made his mission all the more challenging. The work was tedious and there was considerable persecution. Hyde spent much of his time reading the scriptures and praying.

After almost seven years, there were very few conversions and Hyde began to believe he should just lead his fellow missionaries in prayer for the salvation of souls and deep intercession for India. He became so committed to prayer, that by 1899 he began spending entire nights face down before God.

In 1904, Indian Christians and western missionaries gathered for the first of an annual series of conventions at Sialkot in what is today known as Pakistan. To support this time of spiritual renewal, John Hyde and his friends formed the Punjab Prayer Union, setting aside half an hour each day to pray for revival. The results of their prayers were plainly seen at the Sialkot Convention, where a special anointing fell upon those gathered. By the 1908 convention, a growing urgency for evangelism and intercession prevailed among the attendees. John Hyde emerged as the prayer leader, and all were amazed at both the depth of his spiritual insight, and the ferocity of his burden for India.

At that year's convention, John Hyde dared to pray what was to many at the convention an impossible request: that during the coming year in India one soul would be saved every day "Three hundred sixty five people converted, baptized, and publicly confessing Jesus as their Savior."

Prayer accomplished this seemingly impossible task that labor had not rewarded and within the year over 400 souls were saved. By the following convention, John Hyde stood again to ask for more. He doubled the request. "Two souls a day Lord." The next year, the prayers were answered. Eight hundred conversions were recorded that year, and still Hyde showed an unquenchable passion for lost souls.

At the 1910 convention, those around Hyde marveled at his faith, as they witnessed his near violent supplications, "Give me souls, oh God, or I die!" Before the meeting ended, John Hyde revealed that he was again doubling his goal for the coming year. "Four souls a day, and nothing less." During the next twelve months John Hyde's ministry took him throughout India. By now he was known as "Praying Hyde", and his intercession was sought at revivals in Calcutta, Bombay, and other large cities. If on any day four people were not converted, Hyde said at night there would be such a weight on his heart he could not eat or sleep until he had prayed through to victory. The number of new converts continually grew. Thousands were saved.

Hyde was a man like the other great men before him who exercised the Dominion Mandate by praying and believing

God that it was only in the furnace of prayer that the battle of the soul and the battle for souls would truly be won. He believed that if our daily activity in prayer were to be aligned to seek God's agenda for the Earth, that God would exercise His agenda for the Earth in our daily activities. Before he died, he shared what God had shown him:

On the day of prayer, God gave me a new experience. I seemed to be away above our conflict here in the Punjab and I saw God's great battle in all India, and then away out beyond in China, Japan, and Africa. I saw how we had been thinking in narrow circles of our own countries and in our own denominations, and how God was now rapidly joining force to force and line to line, and all was beginning to be one great struggle. That, to me, means the great triumph of Christ. We must exercise the greatest care to be utterly obedient to Him who sees all the battlefield all the time. It is only He who can put each man in the place where his life can count for the most.

The Prayers of Sir Winston Churchill's Intercessor

As prime minister, Sir Winston Churchill rallied the British people during WWII, and led his country from the brink of defeat to victory. However, he had a secret weapon in an intercessor named Major Wellesley Tudor-Pole. Major Tudor-Pole prayed for the nation and during the bombings of WWII, he asked for and received the support and authorization from Sir Winston to call the Nation to a one-minute prayer every day.

People were asked to devote one minute of prayer for peace at nine o'clock each evening. Major Tudor-Pole said:

"There is no power on earth that can withstand the united cooperation on spiritual levels of men and women of goodwill everywhere. It is for this reason that the continued and widespread observance of the Silent Minute is of such vital importance in the interest of human welfare."

The Silent Minute began in 1940 during the blitz on the UK. At the time Major Tudor-Pole told Sir Winston he perceived "an inner request from a high spiritual source that there be a Silent Minute of Prayer for Freedom at 9 pm each evening during the striking of Big Ben. If enough people joined in this gesture of dedicated intent, the tide would turn and the invasion of England would be diverted."

There is great power when we do not look at our human limitations; but instead choose to rely on God's intervention. The Bible says –

"And looking at them Jesus said to them, "With people this is impossible, but with God all things are possible." (Matthew 19:26)

There were many great minds and powerful armies that rose up against the forces of Hitler during the war. But, it is the corporate intercession and exercising of the Dominion

Mandate that got God involved and turned the battle around. An article written at the end of the war emphasized the profound power of this corporate intercession of a nation. In 1945, a British intelligence officer was interrogating a high Nazi official. He asked him why he thought Germany lost the war. His reply was, "During the war, you had a secret weapon for which we could find no counter measure, which we did not understand, but it was very powerful. It was associated with the striking of the Big Ben each evening. I believe you called it the 'Silent Minute.'"

Rees Howell

Rees Howell wasn't just an intercessor who prayed. He prayed with intent and under the inspiration of the Holy Spirit. Indeed, he prayed for nations, for kings, for battles and for the deployment of other intercessors. He was one of the most effective intercessors known to the 20th century. Howells started the Welsh Bible College in Wales and trained up student intercessors who were called upon to intercede with God for the well-being of Britain during World War II. They were able to do in prayer impossible things that set the course of nations, destroyed the plans of Hitler and saved the lives of many.

He wrote in his personal diaries, "Intercession is not substitution for sin. There has only ever been one substitute for a world of sinners, Jesus the Son of God. But intercession so identifies the intercessor with the sufferer that it gives him a prevailing place with God. He moves God. He even causes Him to change His mind. He gains his objective, or rather the Spirit gains it through him." God places great value on the life of an intercessor. He will give such a person power to change the destiny of nations.

And I sought for a man among them, that should make up the hedge, and stand in the gap before me for the land, that I should not destroy it, but I found none... (Ezekiel 22:30)

He believed that travailing prayers moved God! He believed that there is a place in prayer, a place of deep intercession, that when you get there you have entered another realm. You have come to the "grace of faith." The place where faith and grace meet and you have what you have prayed. He believed that persistent prayers would open the door to God's supply and give unlimited access to the one who persisted in prayer. He believed that men and women who would pray until they gained the advantage over the enemy would be endowed with a grace to prevail in prayer and break every spiritual and natural resistance. The Bible says,

Praying always with all prayer and supplication in the Spirit, and watching thereunto with all perseverance and supplication for all saints. (Ephesians 6:18)

Rees Howells trained others to pray and intercede for hours and build stamina in their prayer life. He trained intercessors to pray during specific times of the day and throughout the night to gain the advantage over the enemy in areas identified and revealed as he communicated with the Holy Spirit. His greatest joy was to help intercessors locate their "grace of faith." He taught them that there is a difference between a "prayer warrior" and an intercessor.

A prayer warrior can pray for a thing to be done without necessarily being willing for the answer to come through himself; and he is not even bound to continue in the prayer until it is answered. But an intercessor is responsible to gain his objective, and he can never be free until he has gained whatever he is praying for. He will go to any lengths for the prayer to be answered through himself. But once a position of intercession has been gained, tested and proven, the intercessor can claim all the blessings on that grade, whenever it is God's will for him to do so. There is great power in intercession. Once you know the terrain in the spirit you are able to travel to depths and heights in God. When you have received the counsel of the Lord, your warfare becomes easy. Rees Howells decided that he wouldn't live his life exercising his own will and being independent from God. In fact, He decided the only life that was worth living was one that Christ through the enablement of the Holy Spirit could live in Him. He decided that in order to bring the Kingdom of God to Earth and overrule the kingdoms of this world, he was going to have to first master his domain – his own body. He subjected the flesh as Paul said:

> *"Like an athlete I punish my body, treating it roughly, training it to do what it should, not what it wants to. Otherwise I fear that after enlisting others for the race, I myself might be declared unfit and ordered to stand aside." (1 Corinthians 9:27 TLB)*

He knew through his own various experiences and times of relentless imprecatory prayers resisting the spirit of sickness and death that there was a realm in God that rendered the enemy powerless. He also knew that if he were going to reach that realm, he would have to bring his own desires and human frailties under subjection. He realized that in order to let the Holy Spirit live in Him, he would have to keep his body prepared for a the continual, abiding presence of the Holy Spirit. This is what gave him power in prayer. It is the revelatory power that comes through the vehicle of prayer when we exercise our Dominion Mandate to overrule the power of darkness. He knew that if God revealed in prayer, "pray for the person and they will live"; that his prayers, the Spirit praying through him, would produce the fruit of God's prophetic Word concerning their life. He had become sensitive to God's Voice in cases of sickness during times of interceding for others to the point where he began to pray for a move of healing to move throughout the Body of Christ. He often said during that period, that he believed a new era of healing would break forth in the Christian church. Since that time, the Gift of Healing entered the Church and was a hallmark of the Revivals of the 20th Century.

Rees Howells taught the students of intercession the rules of engagement. He taught them that once they had gained a particular spiritual position in prayer and obtained victory over the enemy in that area, their grace for faith was solid and they could now intercede for others. He believed that the success of our warfare with the enemy would only come if we would wait and adhere to the counsel of the Holy Spirit:

Every purpose is established by counsel: and with good advice make war. (Proverbs 20:18)

He believed that once we gained a victory over the enemy in any area through waiting for the revelation of the Holy Spirit in that area; we would become a weapon to be deployed again and again whenever the Holy Spirit chose to use us as a weapon again in that same area. The Bible says –

*"**Thou art my battle axe and weapons of war: for with thee will I break in pieces the nations, and with thee will I destroy kingdoms;"** (Jeremiah 51:20)*

He said "that is the law of intercession on every level of life, that only so far as we have been tested and proved willing to do a thing ourselves, can we intercede for others. Christ is an Intercessor, because He took the place of each one prayed for. We are never called to intercede for sin, that has been done once and for all; but we are often called to intercede for sinners and their needs, and the Holy Ghost can never 'bind the strong man' through us on a higher level than that in which He has first had victory in us.'" Rees Howells believed in the efficacy of travailing prayers. It is in exercising our Dominion Mandate to bring the Kingdom of God down that we truly become a weapon in the hands of the Lord to destroy the kingdom of darkness. We can be effective in bringing God on the scene if we will labor in prayer. Scripture tells us:

The effectual fervent prayer of a righteous man availeth much.
(James 5:16)

Battle of Dunkirk

In May of 1940 the prime minister of Britain, Neville Chamberlain, had just resigned and Winston Churchill had become his replacement. Adolph Hitler's army had already invaded and conquered Poland, Norway, Denmark, Holland, Luxembourg and Belgium. The French Army, along with large numbers of English soldiers, bravely tried to stop the oncoming enemy army, but after 40 days of fighting, the Allied forces were completely routed. They retreated as far as the English Channel.

Close to 500,000 British and French troops found themselves trapped in a tiny coastal enclave known as Dunkirk, with the advancing German army only 15 miles away and German airplanes already bombing Dunkirk. There seemed to be no hope for the men as they sent out desperate calls for help. They were either going to be killed or imprisoned in a matter of days. Even the military leaders thought little could be done to rescue more than a few thousand men.

In that seemingly impossible situation, the churches in Britain called for a day of prayer to be held on Sunday, May 26.

Rees Howells was training intercessors at the Welsh Bible School in Wales. He wrote these words in his journal entry days before the National Day of Prayer was to be held:

"The world is in a panic today and certainly we would be too unless we were sure the Lord has spoken to us. The destiny of England will be at stake today and tomorrow. In a battle such as we are in today, you cannot trust in a meeting or in feelings. We must go back to what God has told us. There is an enemy that we must keep in check until God does the big thing."

A few days later, Rees Howells wrote, "From a worldly standpoint there is no hope of victory but God has said it… Instead of bad news about our soldiers, if He is on the field of battle, He can change that and make it very good news."

Rees Howells said to his intercessors, "God will not do a bit more through you than you have faith for…You are more responsible for this victory today than the men on that battle field. You must be dead to everything else but this fight. Because you have committed yourself, you are responsible." Look at the training of these intercessors. It is one thing to pray. It is another thing to travail. My prayers can be selfish. To ensure that what I want – lining up with God's Will – is enforced. But, then there are times when what He wants is tantamount and takes precedence and must take preeminence over every other will, including the human appetite and personal connection. When God will wake you up, ask you to give up food, sleep, and worldly pleasures to pray for a people, a nation, a situation that you are not connected to – except by prayer. God looks for people who are willing to stand in the gap and rebuild the broken hedges of protection. These kinds of people are rare and they receive His protection.

> *"And I sought for a man among them, that should make up the hedge, and stand in the gap before me for the land, that I should not destroy it: but I found none." (Ezekiel 22:30)*

There are entire generations that go by without people who are willing to serve and obey God with such selfless abandonment. Thank God for the intercessors in WWII. But, even as they joined in prayer services around Great Britain and other parts of the world, praying for God to intervene, the enemy continued to advance –

Historians say that regardless of the prayers of the people and the historic record number of attendees in church in Great Britain that weekend, Hitler pushed forward and was aggressively on the move to take the territory. The victory looked to be imminent. Dunkirk was bombed and shelled from the air and from a distance. Thunderstorms and thick fog made it difficult for the planes to fly or see, but still Hitler's army continued to advance. However, he did something that to this day is still debated and is called "the turning point of the war." He issued a Halt Order to his forces on May 24th. Against the advice of his own generals, he ordered his army to hold their position. This order permitted time for the Allied Forces to develop a risky plan of evacuation.

Beloved, if you will not be dissuaded by the resistance of the enemy and continue to persist in prayer, I believe we will see a move of God like never before. Some of the greatest revivals broke the atmosphere in the darkest of days. Don't look at how much ground the enemy has taken and how big his territory has become. Focus on how big our God is and that God will use you as a weapon if you will be willing to engage Him in times of intercession and prayer.

That weekend Rees Howells was praying with his intercessors and he told them, "I want to fight with this enemy again this weekend as if it were the end of civilization. You don't leave anything to chance. Don't allow these men at the front to do more than you do here." He was relentless in prayer and he understood that this battle would only be won on their knees.

On the evening of the National Day of Prayer, May 26th, an order was issued for boats of all sizes and shapes to cross the English Channel and rescue as many men as possible. They were asking for these small boats to do what larger boats could not accomplish without great risk. In fact, the large naval ships couldn't even get close to the beaches for rescue, so small boats were critical in transporting men to the larger ships – or all the way to British shores.

Accepting the challenge took tremendous courage for the boat operators. They knew the waters of the English Channel could be extremely dangerous for small boats, and they knew German bombs that caused damage to larger ships would indeed sink them. Above all, they knew that not taking any action at this point in history would have devastating consequences, so they chose to take the risks. During this time the Halt Order had immobilized the German Army. By the time they were on the move again, 336,000 men had already been rescued with little boats and yachts alike, as the rescuers made numerous trips back and forth across the English Channel. The impossible had been accomplished! God had made a way using ordinary men who were willing to take a risk.

Beloved, the Battle of Dunkirk was a battle won by the corporate prayers of a nation, the mobilization of common men willing to do something uncommon and the relentless prayers of those who were willing to lay down their lives for a cause greater than themselves. We cannot expect to win great victories alone. The kingdom of hell is an organized kingdom and evil will not quit until it destroys good. Winning great battles is only possible when good men are galvanized to come together and like the Battle of Dunkirk, take the small that they have and let it be used for the greater good and benefit of all the people.

For every battle of the warrior is with confused noise, and garments rolled in blood; but this shall be with burning and fuel of fire. (Isaiah 9:5)

Lord, send Revival Fires!

Fasts Proclaimed in American History

If my people, which are called by my name, shall humble themselves, and pray, and seek my face, and turn from their wicked ways; then will I hear from heaven, and will forgive their sin, and will heal their land. Now mine eyes shall be open, and mine ears attentive unto the prayer that is made in this place. (2 Chronicles 7:14-15)

The National Day of Prayer in America is an annual day of observance designated by the United States Congress to be held on the first Thursday of May, when people are asked "to turn to God in prayer and meditation." Each year since its inception, the president has signed a proclamation, encouraging all Americans to pray on this day. When we ask God to get involved in the affairs of this Earth, no matter how men have ruled the Earth, God is able to bring His Kingdom on the scene and turn the battle in our favor. Let's look at times of prayer and the results of such calls to action.

The modern law formalizing its annual observance was enacted in 1952, although earlier days of fasting and prayer had been established by the Second Continental Congress from 1775 until 1783, and by President John Adams in 1798 and 1799. Most presidents have issued annual or special occasion proclamations for a national day of prayer, with the notable exceptions of Thomas Jefferson and Andrew Jackson.

Dates and Circumstances American Presidents called for Prayer:

George Washington and the Assembly of Virginia

- Declared: June 1, 1774 as a Day of Fasting, Humiliation and Prayer
- Reason: The British Parliament had ordered an embargo on the port of Boston.
- Result: Victory for the U.S.
- George Washington, the nation's first president, not only believed in praying for divine intervention, but he also believed in acknowledging such interventions when prayer was answered. He declared February 19, 1795 for National Thanksgiving and prayer.

President John Adams

- Declared: May 9, 1798 as a Day of Solemn Humiliation, Fasting and Prayer
- Reason: The United States came to the verge of open war with France
- Result: War was averted

President James Madison

- Declared: January 12, 1815 was to be a Day of Public, Humiliation, Fasting and Prayer to the Almighty God
- Reason: For the safety and welfare of the United States, because the US found itself at war with Britain.
- Result: Four days before the set day, the last battle of this war was fought, resulting in a victory for the U.S. Peace followed shortly afterwards.
- The outcome of this national day of fasting and prayer reflected God's promise given in Isaiah 65:24: "And it

shall come to pass, that before they call, I will answer; and while they are yet speaking, I will hear."
- As a result the second Thursday in April, 1815 was declared a day of Public Thanksgiving.

During the presidency of Abraham Lincoln, three separate days of humiliation, prayer and fasting were proclaimed.

First Fast:

- Last Thursday in September, 1861 as a day of national humiliation, prayer and fasting
- Reason: For the restoration of national peace and unity during the Civil War.

Second Fast:

- Lincoln's second proclamation on the 30th of March, 1863
- Reason: The people of the United States needed to repent as a country through prayer and fasting.

Third Fast:

- First Thursday in August, 1864
- Reason: Cooperation of all who held positions of authority in every area of national life.

If modern America is going to experience Revival, someone is going to have to pray. An intercessor will have to lift up a lamentation for that great nation. If the Lord returns today, will He find faith in America? Will He find someone praying to Him in expectancy of His return? The Lord can do anything. He will avenge us speedily, but only if someone prays and asks Him to get involved.

And he spake a parable unto them to this end, that men ought always to pray, and not to faint.... And shall not God avenge his own elect, which cry day and night unto him, though he bear long with them? I tell you that he will avenge them speedily. Nevertheless when the Son of man cometh, shall he find faith on the earth? (Luke 18:1, 7-8)

National Days of Prayer and Fasting – Great Britain

There were fasting and prayers in Great Britain as early as 1853 for a cholera epidemic. The government proclaimed days of national fasting and humiliation. In 1854, Britons fasted and prayed over the Crimean War, which produced the rise of Florence Nightingale and quality training for nurses caring for the wounded. In 1857, after the Indian Mutiny, the government proclaimed a day for "a Solemn Fast, Humiliation and Prayer before Almighty God; in order to obtain Pardon of our Sins, and for imploring His Blessing and assistance on our arms for the Restoration of Tranquility in India." Most notable are the two fasts during WWII.

1st National Day of Prayer: Sunday, 26 May, 1940

- Reason: For deliverance at a time when Britain was staring military disaster in the face in an area around Dunkirk.

- The King and Queen were present for the main service at Westminster Abbey with the Prime Minister Winston Churchill.
- Result: What became known as 'the miracle of Dunkirk' -- victory by a series of providences, including strategic mistakes by the German command and the helpfulness of the weather.

2nd National Day of Prayer: Sunday, 8 September, 1940

- Reason: The Royal Air Force had taken a pounding from the German Luftwaffe, and Britain seemed to be on the verge of a defeat that would open the door for invasion.
- Results: The previous day had seen the beginning of the blitzkrieg, the horrific German bombing campaign upon civilian London. However, this shift of direction gave relief to the fighter bases and enabled the Royal Air Force to regroup successfully for the climactic weeks of the Battle of Britain.

Today when you go to Great Britain, there is little evidence left of the Great Welsh Revivals that transformed the nation and gave birth to so many other moves of God around the world. Restaurants and stores have replaced many great churches that were once filled with prayers and worship of the Lord Jesus Christ. The great Welsh Revival and the fire that swept through Britain are barely traceable today. Still, I stand convinced by scripture and by experiential knowledge of seeing a move of God birthed by prayer – He can do it again. God will always come where He has been before, if He is invited. Beloved, won't someone get a burden for the United Kingdom? Won't someone take up Great Britain in prayer? Thy Kingdom Come O Lord!

Wilt thou not revive us again: that thy people may rejoice in thee? Shew us thy mercy, O Lord, and grant us thy salvation. (Psalm 85:6-7)

Chapter Summary:

In all these stories of revival, prayer and fasting, corporate repentance on a national level and the move of the Spirit of the Living God, the points we must take away:

- Nothing happens until someone prays
- Revival will not come unless someone is willing to sacrifice in times of prayer
- Even though great men of faith like Smith Wigglesworth and Lester Sumrall prophesied we would see a great revival across the globe, we must pray for it to happen
- No matter how dark the battle seems, God can cause the enemy to "halt" and give us a strategy through prayer that will save the souls of many and we will see the travail of our souls
- **Beloved, nothing happens until someone prays and we will never know how to pray, until we pray! It's time to pray like never before!**

Chapter 4

The Prayers of Abraham

"Can Jesus Christ see the agony of His soul in us? He can't unless we are so closely identified with Him that we have His view concerning the people for whom we pray. May we learn to intercede so wholeheartedly that Jesus Christ will be completely and overwhelmingly satisfied with us as intercessors." – **Oswald Chambers**

Now that we have discussed our role in bringing God on the scene through exercising the Dominion Mandate in prayer and we have looked at men in this dispensation and age of the Church that have been able to bring God on the scene by prayer – now we can look at the Biblical models that we should use to show us how to communicate with God and get Him involved in the affairs of men.

The prayer of Abraham in Genesis 18 is a model prayer for every intercessor. Intercession is standing in the gap for an individual, family, organization, church, city, nation or continent. There are times that Almighty God will seek for an intercessor. An anchor scripture for an intercessor is found in Ezekiel 22:30:

And I sought for a man among them, that should make up the hedge, and stand in the gap before me for the land, that I should not destroy it: but I found none. (Ezekiel 22:30)

God sent Christ when He couldn't find anyone else. Christ gave us the charge when He left that He would be busy praying for us, but that we should pray for the Holy Spirit to come and empower us to be witnesses and bring God on the scene all over the Earth.

"But ye shall receive power, after that the Holy Ghost is come upon you: and ye shall be witnesses unto me both in Jerusalem, and in all Judaea, and in Samaria, and unto the uttermost part of the earth."
(Acts 1:8)

The ministry of intercession is a very high calling that requires many qualities. The intercessor stands between God and man to plead with God on behalf of men. The prayer of intercession requires selflessness, commitment, dedication, persistence, courage and boldness, among many other qualities. It also requires a passion to see the plans and purposes of God manifest.

The responsibility of an intercessor is very serious because the destiny of many depends on the role and faithfulness of an intercessor. The prayer of Abraham in Genesis 18 is a powerful example of intercession.

[17] *And the Lord said, Shall I hide from Abraham that thing which I do;*

[20] *And the Lord said, Because the cry of Sodom and Gomorrah is great, and because their sin is very grievous;*

[21] *I will go down now, and see whether they have done altogether according to the cry of it, which is come unto me; and if not, I will know.*

²² And the men turned their faces from thence, and went toward Sodom: but Abraham stood yet before the Lord.

²³ And Abraham drew near, and said, Wilt thou also destroy the righteous with the wicked?

²⁴ Peradventure there be fifty righteous within the city: wilt thou also destroy and not spare the place for the fifty righteous that are therein?

²⁵ That be far from thee to do after this manner, to slay the righteous with the wicked: and that the righteous should be as the wicked, that be far from thee: Shall not the Judge of all the earth do right?

²⁶ And the Lord said, If I find in Sodom fifty righteous within the city, then I will spare all the place for their sakes.

²⁷ And Abraham answered and said, Behold now, I have taken upon me to speak unto the Lord, which am but dust and ashes:

²⁸ Peradventure there shall lack five of the fifty righteous: wilt thou destroy all the city for lack of five? And he said, If I find there forty and five, I will not destroy it.

²⁹ And he spake unto him yet again, and said, Peradventure there shall be forty found there. And he said, I will not do it for forty's sake.

³⁰ And he said unto him, Oh let not the Lord be angry, and I will speak: Peradventure there shall thirty be found there. And he said, I will not do it, if I find thirty there.

³¹ And he said, Behold now, I have taken upon me to speak unto the Lord: Peradventure there shall be twenty found there. And he said, I will not destroy it for twenty's sake.

³² And he said, Oh let not the Lord be angry, and I will speak yet but this once: Peradventure ten shall be found there. And he said, I will not destroy it for ten's sake.

³³ And the Lord went his way, as soon as he had left communing with Abraham: and Abraham returned unto his place. (Genesis 18:17, 20-33)

This portion of scripture is a vivid example of intercession. God came to Abraham to reveal His plan of destruction for Sodom and Gomorrah and Abraham began to plead with God concerning the two cities. You will realize that there was a very strong relationship between Abraham and God and this relationship gave Abraham the authority to bargain and negotiate with God in prayer.

Now, you can see why constant, earnest prayer – particularly, intercessory prayer – is not only recommended to Christians, it is essential to preempt, end or mitigate earthly suffering; or to bring about a new blessing.

This intercessor has enormous power. The role of an intercessor is to bargain and negotiate with God on behalf of man, as the Prophet Jeremiah tells us.

But if they be prophets, and if the word of the Lord be with them, let them now make intercession to the Lord of hosts, that the vessels which are left in the house of the Lord, and in the house of the king of Judah, and at Jerusalem, go not to Babylon. (Jeremiah 27:18)

Jeremiah declared that the prophets of Judah had the power to overturn the judgment of God, if only they would intercede. God waits to show us mercy if only we would lift up prayer.

In the account of Genesis 18, Abraham had received divine messengers who were going to investigate the condition of the cities to confirm the cries of its inhabitants before God executed judgment over the cities. Abraham, the intercessor, began to plead with God.

Surely the Lord God will do nothing, but he revealeth his secret unto his servants the prophets. (Amos 3:7)

There is always a way God communicates with intercessors. He gives the intercessor who will wait in prayer, advanced knowledge about His plans and purposes and then He begins to empower the intercessor to fulfill His assignment, usually by sending a burden or a prompting to the intercessor from the Holy Spirit. It is not God's desire to always enter into judgment, so He always seeks an intercessor who can skillfully negotiate with Him so that He can avoid judgment.

Judgment is a "strange work" and a "strange act" to God. It is not something that He likes to carry out. God would prefer not to carry out judgment because His nature is that of love, mercy and grace.

"For the Lord shall rise up as in mount Perazim, he shall be wroth as in the valley of Gibeon, that he may do his work, his strange work; and bring to pass his act, his strange act." (Isaiah 28:21)

It is God's intent for us to be blessed, but the enemy knows that sin produces the wrath of God, which results in judgment. The role of the intercessor is to appease the wrath of God, plead for mercy and avert His judgment. That is why the Bible says of Christ:

Wherefore he is able also to save them to the uttermost that come unto God by him, seeing he ever liveth to make intercession for them. (Hebrews 7:25)

The throne of God is known as the Throne of Grace and this reveals the nature of God. He is a God of love, grace and mercy and because of His nature, He is always looking for an intercessor to reason and plead with Him so that He can demonstrate mercy and grace. He is also a God of justice.

If we confess our sins, He is faithful and righteous to forgive us our sins and to cleanse us from all unrighteousness. (1 John 1:9)

Because He is a just God, He must also punish wrong. He needs an intercessor to plead with him to show mercy instead of punishing wrong. We should always believe and pray that mercy will triumph over judgment for the righteous. We must also learn to pray and execute the judgment written over the wicked and the powers of darkness. It is in the power of the righteous to execute God's plan for the wicked.

There is a difference between the wicked and the sinner and the Bible shows us that God makes this distinction. He has a plan for and will save the sinner who repents.

But God commendeth his love toward us, in that, while we were yet sinners, Christ died for us. (Romans 5:8)

God's plan for the wicked is not the same as His plan for the sinner.

Thou hast rebuked the heathen, thou hast destroyed the wicked, thou hast put out their name for ever and ever. (Psalm 9:5)

But the transgressors shall be destroyed together: the end of the wicked shall be cut off. (Psalm 37:38)

But, in differentiating between sinners and the wicked, the most telling Scripture is found in Psalm 1:4-5:

The wicked are not so, But are like the chaff which the wind driveth away. Therefore the wicked shall not stand in the judgment, Nor sinners in the congregation of the righteous.

The Hebrew word "*rasha*" (translated in the above passage as "wicked") means one who is hostile to God. It is sometimes translated as "ungodly." It describes those who are aware of God, but choose to act contrary and against Him, selling themselves out to willingly do what they know is contrary to God's plan for mankind. He will destroy them like chaff on the Day of Judgment. Our assignment on Earth is to oppose such people. Just as God needs a body to execute His plan in the Earth, so does evil need a body to execute wicked assignments from the powers of darkness. So, it is the righteous through exercising our Dominion Mandate, we execute the judgment written against the wicked. Again, see how the scripture denotes a different standing – or position – for the wicked and for sinners:

The wicked are not so, But are like the chaff which the wind driveth away. Therefore the wicked shall not stand in the judgment, Nor sinners in the congregation of the righteous. (Psalm 1:4-5)

The Hebrew word "*chatta*" (translated in the above scripture as "sinner") describes someone who is counted as guilty for their offenses and, from God's point of view, ready for condemnation. The warning here is that the sinner will be exempted from the congregation of the righteous – so we must repent from sin. That means that we must resolve to live holy -- to be counted among the righteous -- or we risk separation from God. Our assignment is to pray for such people that they would receive a revelation of Christ.

We know that God heareth not sinners: but if any man be a worshipper of God, and do his will, him he heareth. (John 9:31)

God wants us to pray for the lost and to call them to repentance. That is the assignment of the intercessor. You cannot be both an accuser of the brethren and an intercessor at the same time. You must pray for others to come into the Kingdom.

"And he said unto them, The harvest indeed is plenteous, but the laborers are few: pray ye therefore the Lord of the harvest, that he send forth laborers into his harvest."(Luke 10:2)

"Brethren, if anyone among you wanders from the truth, and someone turns him back, let him know that he who turns a sinner from the error of his way will save a soul from death and cover a multitude of sins." (James 5:19-20)

The ministry of intercession is dear to the heart of God because, by His own volition, God cannot carry out His purposes here in the Earth realm. He has instituted and established laws that He cannot alter or break.

In Chapter 2, we discussed the Dominion Mandate and that God's original plan was for Man to govern the affairs of men in the Earth. He delegated His own authority to man as it relates to the governance of the Earth.

The heavens are the Lord's heavens, but the earth he has given to the children of man.

(Psalm 115:16)

The God Head sat in counsel and through an eternal judicial determination, decided to make man in their image and after their likeness. They did not end there. They went on to determine that they would give man dominion over everything in the Earth realm. When God decreed to "let them have dominion," He subjected Himself to His Word, despite his rulership. He put all of creation under the dominion of man. It is not that He is not capable or able. It is that in His infinite Wisdom and Divine Plan, this is the order He has set in place. The psalmist said:

"What is man, that thou art mindful of him? and the son of man, that thou visitest him? For thou hast made him a little lower than the Elohim, and hast crowned him with glory and honour. Thou madest him to have dominion over the works of thy hands; thou hast put all things under his feet." (Psalms 8:4-6)

When God gave man dominion over the earth, it meant that no other created being had the authority to function in the Earth realm without man's permission or invitation. Indeed God created man with his own will – allowing the man to receive Him or to resist Him. In giving dominion to man, He also made Himself subject to His Word. This can be hard for a believer to accept. However, repeatedly scripture tells us God subjected Himself and that He can be influenced by His Word being recapitulated by a believer using the authority of the Dominion Mandate. <u>God will respond to us when we put Him in remembrance of His Word.</u>

It is important to remember that at the stage of creation when God gave man the Dominion Mandate, the man God was referring to was made in His image and His likeness. When God made this decree in Genesis 1, He was referring to the spirit of man.

God is a spirit; so the man that God was communicating with is the spirit man. The body of man had not yet been formed. The body of man was formed in Genesis 2.

And the Lord God formed man of the dust of the ground, and breathed into his nostrils the breath of life; and man became a living soul. (Genesis 2:7)

God gave dominion to the spirit man. When He gave mankind dominion, the issue of gender had also not been addressed because it was after the decision and the decree, "Let them have dominion", that He made them male and female. God was not speaking to the flesh, but to the spirit.

We cannot know Him or His Will in the flesh, we must know Him in the Spirit. This is why the Word declares:

"For what man knoweth the things of a man, save the spirit of man which is in him? even so the things of God knoweth no man, but the Spirit of God. Now we have received, not the spirit of the world, but the spirit which is of God; that we might know the things that are freely given to us of God." (1 Cor. 2:11-12)

These details are very important to establish a very strong foundation for prayer because you will realize from these scriptures that God cannot do anything in the earth realm until someone invites Him. This is why prayer is so important and critical for the establishment of the purposes of God.

When God said, "*Let them have dominion*," it meant that, in His eternal wisdom and counsel, He had given the dominion of the earth to man. He didn't have it, man now had it and whatever man allowed was what was going to be allowed in the earth realm.

This places a lot of responsibility on the intercessor because, through prayer and intercession, we allow or disallow God to intervene in the events in the Earth realm. This is why Scripture speaks about what you bind on Earth shall be bound in Heaven and what you loose on Earth will be loosed in Heaven.

And I will give unto thee the keys of the kingdom of heaven: and whatsoever thou shalt bind on earth shall be bound in heaven: and whatsoever thou shalt loose on earth shall be loosed in heaven. (Matthew 16:19)

These scriptures reveal the level of authority that God gave to man. It is important for you to know that dominion has been given to you and you need to exercise it so that through prayer and intercession, you can allow the Hand of God to intervene in the affairs of humanity.

The story of Abraham's intercession on behalf of the cities of Sodom and Gomorrah reveals vividly the amount of power the intercessor has. If Abraham had continued his intercession and not stopped at ten people, the judgment of those cities would have been averted. You have this same power when you exercise the Dominion Mandate. Your prayers have power to move God!

It is time for you to go to God in intercession. God is counting on you for the destiny of many. You cannot afford to allow the flesh, tiredness or weariness to hinder you. You also do not want to stop the intercession until you sense a complete note of victory.

The first Adam failed by remaining silent while the enemy brought deception and chaos. God did not come and restore order. Instead, He had already prepared the Second Adam. Jesus Christ is "The Lamb" that was slain before the foundation of the Earth.

As intercessors, we enforce the purpose for which Christ came: to restore God's original plan of dominion to man.

After that the end will come when he will turn the Kingdom over to God the Father, having put down all enemies of every kind. For Christ will be King until he has defeated all his enemies, including the last enemy—death. This too must be defeated and ended. For the rule and authority over all things has been given to Christ by his Father; except, of course, Christ does not rule over the Father himself, who gave him this power to rule. When Christ has finally won the battle against all his enemies, then he, the Son of God, will put himself also under his Father's orders, so that God who has given him the victory over everything else will be utterly supreme. (1 Corinthians 15:24-28)

This Scripture tells us that God will not be utterly supreme in this world until we enforce the judgment written. He left us power and authority in order that we might enforce the judgment written in Revelation 11:15:

And the seventh angel sounded; and there were great voices in heaven, saying, The kingdoms of this world are become the kingdoms of our Lord, and of his Christ; and he shall reign for ever and ever.

Chapter Summary:

- Genesis 18 is a Biblical model for intercession
- God saw fit to reveal His plans to Abraham because Abraham was an intercessor
- God looks for an intercessor to stand in the gap before He executes judgment
- Judgment, even when mandated, is a strange act to God because His nature is love, grace and mercy. That is why He looks for someone to stand in the gap for mankind
- There is a difference between the wicked and the sinner. There is a judgment for the wicked, but mercy

is available to sinners. The difference is connected to the intent behind the behavior.
- Wicked people (*rasha*) are hostile toward God and choose to destroy good people, often relying on the assistance of dark powers that work behind the scenes. They are in partnership with evil. Wicked is never satisfied until good is destroyed.
- Sinners (*chatta*) are guilty and stained with sin and acts of unrighteousness. We can intercede for sinners and when we sin we can repent and God will show us mercy and deliver us from evil.
- When God gave man the Dominion Mandate, He was speaking to the Spirit of man. We cannot intercede in the flesh. We must intercede by the power of the Holy Spirit.
- The keys to bind and loose are keys of Revelation that we obtain in Spirit-led times of prayer.
- Intercessors have the power to bring God on the scene in the affairs of the Earth.

Chapter 5

The Prayers of Moses

> *"What the Church needs to-day is not more machinery or better, not new organizations or more and novel methods, but men whom the Holy Ghost can use -- men of prayer, men mighty in prayer. The Holy Ghost does not flow through methods, but through men. He does not come on machinery, but on men. He does not anoint plans, but men -- men of prayer."* – **E.M. Bounds, Power Through Prayer**

In this chapter, you will encounter a man that had the ability to move God because of His prayers. Moses is a man who God used to bring reformation to a nation. Through his prayers and his actions taken after times and seasons with God – in one day, through one divine instruction, power changed hands. The nation of Egypt was driven to bankruptcy overnight and the nation of Israel became wealthy on the same night. God responds to the heartfelt prayers of intercession when we ask Him to get involved in the affairs of men. This is our ability to exercise the Dominion Mandate.

Moses was so powerful in intercession; the scriptures say He caused God to repent. He asked in deep intercession – and God changed His mind. Let's read the account in Exodus 32:

⁷ And the Lord said unto Moses, Go, get thee down; for thy people, which thou broughtest out of the land of Egypt, have corrupted themselves:

⁸ They have turned aside quickly out of the way which I commanded them: they have made them a molten calf, and have worshipped it, and have sacrificed thereunto, and said, These be thy gods, O Israel, which have brought thee up out of the land of Egypt.

⁹ And the Lord said unto Moses, I have seen this people, and, behold, it is a stiffnecked people:

¹⁰ Now therefore let me alone, that my wrath may wax hot against them, and that I may consume them: and I will make of thee a great nation.

¹¹ And Moses besought the Lord his God, and said, Lord, why doth thy wrath wax hot against thy people, which thou hast brought forth out of the land of Egypt with great power, and with a mighty hand?

¹² Wherefore should the Egyptians speak, and say, For mischief did he bring them out, to slay them in the mountains, and to consume them from the face of the earth? Turn from thy fierce wrath, and repent of this evil against thy people.

¹³ Remember Abraham, Isaac, and Israel, thy servants, to whom thou didst swear by thine own self, and sadist unto them, I will multiply your seed as the stars of heaven, and all this land that I have spoken of will I give unto your seed, and they shall inherit it forever.

¹⁴ And the Lord repented of the evil which he thought to do unto his people. (Exodus 32:7-14)

In order to understand our role as Intercessors and the weight of authority we can carry in times of praying for others, for families, for churches, for nations or anything the Spirit asks that we are being given a role of great responsibility and we should learn from the life of Moses. Moses was a man who God spoke to face to face as a man speaks to his friend.

"And the Lord spake unto Moses face to face, as a man speaketh unto his friend…." (Exodus 33:11)

The influence of Moses with God was very powerful and this reveals the kind of influence that a praying person can have with God. In the prayer of Moses we just read, you see Moses reminding God of His covenant with Abraham, Isaac and Jacob and telling God to repent of the evil He had planned. And the scripture reveals, "the Lord repented of the evil which He had thought to do against His people." What a powerful revelation of one man exercising his dominion in prayer. God restrained Himself because of the prayers of Moses.

It is important as an intercessor for you to know the Word and promises of God. Moses knew how to put God in remembrance of His Word and to lift His Word up to Him in prayer. Whenever you approach God, you must approach Him on the basis of his Word.

__Put me in remembrance: let us plead together: declare thou, that thou mayest be justified. (Isaiah 43:26)__

Moses reminded God of His covenant with Abraham, Isaac and Jacob and on the basis of the promises of God, he was able to get God to change His mind over and over in order to get the people closer to the land of promise. Whenever you come before God, you must put Him in remembrance of His Word and He will respond on the basis of His Word.

The prayers of Moses reveal the influence and power that the prayers of the saints have with God. God responded to the prayers of Moses. It is important for you to know that God does answer and respond to the prayers of His people. He wants to get involved; He is always looking for an intercessor.

There are a few things you can learn from the prayers of Moses:

1. He heard from God
2. He had a dynamic and intimate relationship with God.
3. He knew the covenants and plans of God.

The Lord spoke to Moses and gave Moses instructions concerning His people. Then God said to Moses, "Let me alone," which implies that Moses' relationship with God and His prayers restrained God from doing what He originally wanted to do. "Let me alone" literally means that Moses was holding God back!

For Almighty God to tell one man "Let me alone" shows the levels of influence and power that man had with God. It reveals the respect and honor that God has for His servants. It is important for you to realize that God is a spirit and He is the creator of the universe and for the creator of the universe to be seeking permission from a man before He carries out his operations reveals the strength of the Dominion Mandate.

The above scriptures demonstrate that God abides by the laws He put in place for humanity to have dominion in the Earth realm.

The dialogue between God and Moses is very revealing and it speaks volumes to the present day believer and intercessor of how much influence and power one can have with God. The destiny of a nation was in the balance yet one man had so much power with God. You can walk in that level of power and authority with God through your prayer life.

The scriptures declare that whatsoever was written aforetime was written for our learning that through the patience and comfort of the scriptures we might have hope. (Romans 15: 4)

As you read these powerful examples of prayer, I know that faith is being ignited in your spirit and fresh revelation is being imparted to you. This dialogue between Moses and God immediately reveals the power and influence of prayer. If at any time you have had doubts about whether God hears and answers prayer, this portion of Scripture gives a clear picture about how God responds to prayer.

A man could tell God to repent and God repented. Moses said to God "repent of this thy evil which thou hadst against thy people" and God repented. Look at Exodus 32:11-14 again and meditate on the exchange between God and Moses. Are you willing to intercede for the destiny of others to be delivered? Can you stay in the furnace of prayer until your heartfelt prayers have changed the fate of another person?

These are very powerful statements pregnant with divine revelation and I sincerely believe that your life and the destiny of all those you were created to influence would go through an amazing transformation once you grasp the depth of this revelation.

The Lord's response to a man was determining the destiny of an entire nation. One man's prayer had so much power to change the mind of God. I am sure that you are beginning to realize how much power and influence your prayer has. If the enemy ever deceived you into believing that it is a waste of time to pray or that prayer is not important or effective, these Scriptures reveal something completely different.

"And the Lord repented of the evil he thought to do unto His people." He changed his mind! A man could approach God with the counsel of God and remind God of His covenant promises to His covenant people and God changed His mind about the actions He was about to take.

Moses was such a powerful example of a prophetic intercessor that the scriptures write of him –

Since that time no prophet has risen in Israel like Moses, whom the LORD knew face to face, for all the signs and wonders which the LORD sent him to perform in the land of Egypt against Pharaoh, all his servants, and all his land, and for all the mighty power and for all the great terror which Moses performed in the sight of all Israel."
(Deuteronomy 34:10-12)

Moses was a man who obeyed God and was willing to stand in the gap for a nation. Because of that, he was deemed to be the greatest prophet to ever rise in that nation.

Could you be called to prophetic intercession for your nation? Are you willing to do what it takes to be a weapon in the Hand of God? What will people write about your prayer life after you have left the Earth?

About 19 years ago, I was preaching at the church of a friend, Dr. Leo Cullimore in the Virgin Islands. I was then staying at the Sugar Bay Hotel. Hurricane Louise was seen moving with great force towards the island. As I stayed up through the night to pray, at midnight I was led by the Holy Spirit to rebuke, block and avert the storm and I did. The storm responded to prayer; was averted and the island was saved from great destruction. Praise the Lord.

You too can approach God in prayer and remind him of His word and covenant promises and God will honor His word. Prayer is powerful and the prayers of the righteous have tremendous influence in the realm of the spirit.

It is time for you to rise up and pray strategic prayers under the influence and guidance of the Holy Spirit and you will experience the manifestation of the plans and purposes of God.

Chapter Summary:

Moses prayed using great strategy in prayer and it moved God. We must pray through the power and revelation of the

Holy Spirit if we are going to see success in our prayer life. Strategic prayers:

- Must be made to exercise our Dominion Mandate.
- Must be made to establish the plans and purposes of God.
- Must be made to overrule every projection of the enemy.
- Are required for the demolishing of strongholds of the enemy.
- Are required for divine intervention in critical moments.
- Are required for community and national transformation.
- Are required for financial breakthroughs and miracles.
- Are required for the advancement of the Kingdom of God.

Chapter 6

The Prayers of Elijah

*"Our prayers lay the track down which God's power can come. Like a mighty locomotive, his power is irresistible, but it cannot reach us without rails." – **Watchman Nee***

The spirit of Elijah and the mantles of Elijah are still available to this generation. These are mantles of governmental authority that bring into manifestation the acts and miracles of God. It is when we exercise the Dominion Mandate that we walk in governmental authority and bring solutions from the throne room perspective to govern the affairs of the Earth. In this chapter you are going to discover from the Scriptures how God responds to persistent prayers and how the promises and prophecies of God are brought into manifestation.

1 Kings 18 provides a graphic description of the prayers of Elijah. In the book of James, chapter 5 there is a summary of the prophet's prayers:

> ***Elias was a man subject to like passions as we are, and he prayed earnestly that it might not rain: and it rained not on the earth by the space of three years and six months. And he prayed again, and the heaven gave rain, and the earth brought forth her fruit. (James 5:17-18)***

It is important for you to realize that when Elijah made a declaration to King Ahab that there would be no rain (1 Kings 17), the Scriptures did not reveal that Elijah had spent a lot of time praying earnestly that it would not rain. The Scriptures only reveal Elijah appearing on the spiritual, political and socio-economic scene of Israel at a very critical time in the history of the nation – a time when the nation was in a great dilemma.

The covenant children of God were torn between the worship of Baal and the worship of Jehovah. Ahab, king of Israel, had married Jezebel, the daughter of Ethbaal, the king of Zidon. The Zidonians worshipped Baal, so Jezebel came into Israel with her gods. As queen, she had wooed Ahab into Baal worship and he in turn had influenced the nation to turn away from Jehovah, the only true and living God.

[31] And it came to pass, as if it had been a light thing for him to walk in the sins of Jeroboam the son of Nebat, that he took to wife Jezebel the daughter of Ethbaal king of the Zidonians, and went and served Baal, and worshipped him.

[32] And he reared up an altar for Baal in the house of Baal, which he had built in Samaria.

[33] And Ahab made a grove; and Ahab did more to provoke the Lord God of Israel to anger than all the kings of Israel that were before him. (1 Kings 16:31-33)

The nation was in a great state of confusion because of the worship of Baal. It was at this time that Elijah appeared on the scene to declare the word of the Lord.

And Elijah the Tishbite, who was of the inhabitants of Gilead, said unto Ahab, As the Lord God of Israel liveth, before whom I stand,

there shall not be dew nor rain these years, but according to my word.
(1 Kings 17:1)

It is important for you to realize that according to the book of James, Elijah prayed earnestly that it not rain and it did not rain for three and a half years. Later, he prayed for rain and the heavens gave forth rain. The book of 1 Kings does not reveal how intensively Elijah prayed to hold back the rain but does reveal how intensively he prayed for the release of the rain. The account is written in 1 Kings 18:30-39 and continues in 1 Kings 18:41-46:

³⁰ And Elijah said unto all the people, Come near unto me. And all the people came near unto him. And he repaired the altar of the Lord that was broken down.

³¹ And Elijah took twelve stones, according to the number of the tribes of the sons of Jacob, unto whom the word of the Lord came, saying, Israel shall be thy name:

³² And with the stones he built an altar in the name of the Lord: and he made a trench about the altar, as great as would contain two measures of seed.

³³ And he put the wood in order, and cut the bullock in pieces, and laid him on the wood, and said, Fill four barrels with water, and pour it on the burnt sacrifice, and on the wood.

³⁴ And he said, Do it the second time. And they did it the second time. And he said, Do it the third time. And they did it the third time.

³⁵ And the water ran round about the altar; and he filled the trench also with water.

³⁶ And it came to pass at the time of the offering of the evening sacrifice, that Elijah the prophet came near, and said, Lord God of Abraham, Isaac, and of Israel, let it be known this day that thou art God in Israel, and that I am thy servant, and that I have done all these things at thy word.

³⁷ Hear me, O Lord, hear me, that this people may know that thou art the Lord God, and that thou hast turned their heart back again.

³⁸ Then the fire of the Lord fell, and consumed the burnt sacrifice, and the wood, and the stones, and the dust, and licked up the water that was in the trench.

³⁹ And when all the people saw it, they fell on their faces: and they said, The Lord, he is the God; the Lord, he is the God. (1 Kings 18:30-39)

⁴⁰ And Elijah said unto them, Take the prophets of Baal; let not one of them escape. And they took them: and Elijah brought them down to the brook Kishon, and slew them there.

⁴¹ And Elijah said unto Ahab, Get thee up, eat and drink; for there is a sound of abundance of rain.

⁴² So Ahab went up to eat and to drink. And Elijah went up to the top of Carmel; and he cast himself down upon the earth, and put his face between his knees,

⁴³ And said to his servant, Go up now, look toward the sea. And he went up, and looked, and said, There is nothing. And he said, Go again seven times.

⁴⁴ And it came to pass at the seventh time, that he said, Behold, there ariseth a little cloud out of the sea, like a man's hand. And he said, Go up, say unto Ahab, Prepare thy chariot, and get thee down, that the rain stop thee not.

⁴⁵ And it came to pass in the meanwhile, that the heaven was black with clouds and wind, and there was a great rain. And Ahab rode, and went to Jezreel.

⁴⁶ And the hand of the Lord was on Elijah; and he girded up his loins, and ran before Ahab to the entrance of Jezreel. (1 Kings 18:41-46)

In this prayer, Elijah was enforcing a Covenant promise regarding the heavens. He was enforcing the judgment written.

When the children of Israel were on their way to their promised land, caught between their past and their future, God entered into covenant with them. In that covenant, He made it clear to them that if they would obey His voice and serve Him, He would open their heavens and send down rain to them and they would prosper. However, if they would not obey Him, He would shut up their heavens, their ground would be barren and there would be no rain.

¹³ And it shall come to pass, if ye shall hearken diligently unto my commandments which I command you this day, to love the Lord your God, and to serve him with all your heart and with all your soul,

¹⁴ That I will give you the rain of your land in his due season, the first rain and the latter rain, that thou mayest gather in thy corn, and thy wine, and thine oil.

¹⁵ And I will send grass in thy fields for thy cattle, that thou mayest eat and be full.

¹⁶ Take heed to yourselves, that your heart be not deceived, and ye turn aside, and serve other gods, and worship them;

¹⁷ And then the Lord's wrath be kindled against you, and he shut up the heaven, that there be no rain, and that the land yield not her fruit; and lest ye perish quickly from off the good land which the Lord giveth you. (Deuteronomy 11:13-17)

These terms of the covenant that God spoke through Moses were the prayers that Elijah was enforcing in the book of Kings. Elijah prayed earnestly that it would not rain in accordance with the terms of the covenant.

The children of Israel had turned aside and were worshipping Baal so Elijah prayed that God will shut the heavens and that is what happened. The heavens were shut for three and a half years. The intensity with which he prayed for the heavens to open after he heard the prophetic word was the same intensity with which he had prayed for the heavens to be shut.

Elijah was a man of supernatural faith. He had power over the elements. He could call down rain and he could call down fire. The Scriptures declare that he was a man of passions like you and I, but still he prayed earnestly. This means he prayed with intensity and persistence. It is persistence that will break resistance.

When the word of the Lord came to him that God was going to send rain upon the Earth, he went up to the top of Mount Carmel and put his face between his knees and began to travail in prayer. He took a birth position. The prophecies and promises of God have to be birthed through strong, persistent and prevailing prayers. Please remember that nothing happens until someone prays. Prayer moves God!

When Elijah told his servant to go and check if there was any sign of rain, the servant went and came back and informed him that there was no sign of rain. Even though the answer was negative, he did not accept the negative report because he had heard the word of the Lord. He told his servant to go seven times.

You must realize that Elijah's servant had a three-day journey each time he went from the top of Carmel to where he could see the gathering of the clouds. He had to go and come back seven times until he could see a little cloud shaped like a man's fist. For 21 days, Elijah was in persistent prayers, engaging the heavens and demanding that the word of the Lord would come to pass.

The prayers of Elijah are prayers of great faith because anytime the servant came back, his response was negative, yet Elijah still held onto the word of the Lord and prayed until there was a manifestation of the prophetic word.

The prayers of Elijah are inspirational. They encourage us to apply spiritual principles that work for all time. These are governmental prayers that release into manifestation the plans and purposes of God.

The prayers of Elijah reveal the level of coordination between Heaven and Earth that are required for the plans of Heaven to be demonstrated in the Earth realm. This is why we must pray by revelation to enforce the Dominion Mandate. It is this continual communication with the Lord that affords us the opportunity to know His plans and execute His desires in the Earth. The servant said, "I can see a cloud like the fist of a man." The hand of a man was moving the Hand of God to bring the purposes of God into manifestation. Always remember that nothing happens until someone prays and God can do nothing for humanity until someone prays.

On July 1, 2015, I issued a clarion call to men and women in regions all over Ghana to pray for the nation. Among many things, we prayed for the rise of the national currency, the cedi. For over a year, I had been praying this prayer to national and even global ridicule. Believers and unbelievers alike mocked me in local papers and on national radio programs. At one point, an international publication, *The Wall Street Journal,* sent a reporter to write a story on the preacher who was praying for the recovery of the national currency.

Despite that mockery, I kept calling for the rise of the cedi and for God to intervene in the financial condition of Ghana. Would God respond to prayer for economic recovery?

On July 1, the exchange rate of the cedi to the U.S. dollar was 4:3. A week later, the dollar had fallen and the cedi had risen to an exchange rate of 3:4. You do the math. Prayer moves God!

Many people will tell you about the natural things that they believe influence the valuation of the cedi and other world currency. But, world currency is a major component of Biblical prophecy. Currency fluctuations and economic changes are driven by satanic powers. Later in this book when we discuss the hierarchy of Satan's kingdom, we will uncover the powers that influence leaders to take decisions that affect market fluctuation in order to control the kingdoms of the world. It is Biblical prophecy describing the end times that most clearly tells us what their assignment is:

"He also forced everyone, small and great, rich and poor, free and slave, to receive a mark on his right hand or on his forehead, so that no one could buy or sell unless he had the mark, which is the name of the beast or the number of his name." (Revelation 13:16-17)

Biblical prophecy about currency reveals that in the end of time and prior to the return of Christ, Israel will become a very rich nation in gold and silver. These precious metals also must rise in value enough to move other nations to envy so that they will be led to invade Israel at the start of the tribulation. (Ezekiel 38-39.)

A great deal of issues related to currency in gold and oil rich nations are in line with the fulfillment of prophecy. I am not an economist, but I am an intercessor. I pray as the Holy Spirit dictates; and I was moved to pray for the cedi for a long period of time and will continue to pray as the Spirit leads me.

The mockery of men does not move me. In Revelation 3 when Jesus is speaking to the Laodiceans, He rebukes them for being lukewarm and lured into the deception that they are in control of their wealth. They think they are rich and in need of nothing. But, Jesus reveals their true condition and gives them this advice:

> *"Because thou sayest, I am rich, and increased with goods, and have need of nothing; and knowest not that thou art wretched, and miserable, and poor, and blind, and naked: I counsel thee to buy of me gold tried in the fire, that thou mayest be rich; and white raiment, that thou mayest be clothed, and that the shame of thy nakedness do not appear; and anoint thine eyes with eyesalve, that thou mayest see." (Revelation 3:18)*

Beloved, the world we live in today is experiencing an unprecedented time of nations in financial turmoil. Large countries with major currency devaluations and severe economic collapse are destined to fall into financial ruin in order to bring about the chaos that will humble the nations into accepting one world currency and world rule by the antichrist. This will cause God to bring judgment on the world. While I want Christ to come, I know that it is only through intercession (remember how Abraham interceded for Sodom and Gomorrah) that we are able to hold back God's judgment so that men can be saved and the Lord will show us mercy instead of judgment. Say what you want, but I will exercise the Dominion Mandate in prayer and pray for the souls of men, the redemption of my country and the coming revival of the world.

The reason the world economy shakes is so that the wealth of the wicked will come into the hands of the Church in the Earth. Wealth must come to build the church. Scripture says

"And I will shake all nations, <u>and the desire of all nations shall come</u>: and I will fill this house with glory, saith the Lord of hosts. The silver is mine, and the gold is mine, saith the Lord of hosts. The glory of this latter house shall be greater than of the former, saith the Lord of hosts: and in this place will I give peace, saith the Lord of hosts. (Haggai 2:7-9)

In this scripture the "desire of all nations" is peace. Peace is a person and His name is the Prince of Peace. Intercession initiates the shaking of the wealth of nations. In one night the wealth of Egypt was pillaged by the people of God in order for them to serve God's purpose. This plan of God was set in motion through Moses' intercession:

"And I will give this people favour in the sight of the Egyptians: and it shall come to pass, that, when ye go, ye shall not go empty: But every woman shall borrow of her neighbour, and of her that sojourneth in her house, jewels of silver, and jewels of gold, and raiment: and ye shall put them upon your sons, and upon your daughters; and ye shall spoil the Egyptians." (Exodus 3:21-22)

When I look in the faces of those suffering in my country because of the economy, the bowels of my compassion are opened and I am lead to intercede for relief from Heaven. That is why I pray for the currency and economy of nations and I will keep on praying.

Hereby perceive we the love of God, because he laid down his life for us: and we ought to lay down our lives for the brethren. But whoso hath this world's good, and seeth his brother have need, and shutteth up his bowels of compassion from him, how dwelleth the love of God in him. (1 John 3:16-17)

Chapter Summary:

- When nations resort to their own governance, it is the responsibility of the Church to pray and ask for the Kingdom of God to be superimposed over the kingdoms of this world. We do this using our Dominion Mandate in prayer and through the power of Spiritual Revelation.

- We must pray governmental prayers that release the manifestation of the plans and purposes of God into the affairs that govern every nation we find ourselves

- Elijah's prayers took him to the top of Mount Carmel – this caused him to ascend in the spirit. We must be willing to go up and seek God through the power of the Holy Spirit.

- His prayers led him to cast himself down to the Earth – spiritual humility. It is not our power in prayer that moves God. It is a heart of humility that seeks God and acknowledges that we cannot do anything without His help.

- He put his face between his knees – focus and travailing prayers. It is in the furnace of prayer, when we block out all distractions and remove anything that would affect our ability to hear and see what God is saying that we qualify to truly hear and see what God wants to do and receive spiritual insight and revelation.

- He sent his servant to watch and pray. We are commanded to watch and pray. We must stand as watchman and not let the world dictate to us more than we are lead by the scriptures to govern the affairs of the Earth.

- He refused to take no for an answer. He was consistent in prayer until He saw the revelation that He heard in prayer. We must be persistent if we are going to destroy the resistance of the enemy.

- He prayed until he received a breakthrough. Once you hear what the Spirit is saying, do not allow room for unbelief, doubt or discouragement – keep pressing until you get the breakthrough.

- He saw the manifestation of the prophetic word because he was willing to remain in the posture of prayer and keep the faith until he saw the promise. We must remain in faith until there is a manifestation of prophecy.

- God owns the silver and the gold of nations. His Kingdom is not a kingdom without finances. But, we must pray that the righteous take ownership of the silver and the gold in order to establish the church and reveal His Kingdom in every nation where they find themselves.

Chapter 7

The Prayers of Esther

"Every child of God is located where God has placed him for some purpose, and the practical use of this first point is to lead you to enquire for what practical purpose has God placed each one of you where you now are?" – **Charles Spurgeon**

This is the story of an orphan girl who had risen to prominence through divine providence. This is a story of the providence of God. He has placed each one of us in a divine position in the Earth that when we exercise our Dominion Mandate, it permits Him to operate in and through us to enforce the dictates and decrees of the Kingdom of God and overthrow the plans and schemes of the Kingdom of Darkness. God positions each one of us at a particular place, in a particular time and for a particular purpose. He will move through us at the appointed season when we yield to Him and exercise the Dominion Mandate. You are not a mistake, you are not an accident and you are divinely positioned to fulfill God's original intent.

Vashti, who was the queen, had refused to obey the king's command and she had lost her position as queen. Shortly afterwards, the palace conducted a search for beautiful virgins to replace Queen Vashti. The woman who most pleased the King would be the new queen.

Many women, including a motherless and fatherless girl named Esther, were brought to the citadel of Susa, where they were provided special treatment and a special diet. On the advice of her uncle, Mordecai, Esther hid her Jewish and eventually received the favor of Hegai, one of the attendants. She was assigned seven special attendants and received special food and beauty treatments. King Xerxes was attracted to Esther more than any other woman and she eventually won his favor and approval over the other girls and was declared queen.

Working in the palace at Shushan, Mordecai found out about a plot instigated by Haman, by one of the king's advisers, to kill all of the Jews in the land. Mordecai approached Esther with an idea of how she could help thwart Haman's plot. At first, Queen Esther hesitated, protesting that she wasn't qualified to be of any real help. Mordecai saw her hesitation and even though she was his beloved niece, he told her the stark truth.

¹³ Then Mordecai commanded to answer Esther, Think not with thyself that thou shalt escape in the king's house, more than all the Jews.

¹⁴ For if thou altogether holdest thy peace at this time, then shall there enlargement and deliverance arise to the Jews from another place; but thou and thy father's house shall be destroyed: and who knoweth whether thou art come to the kingdom for such a time as this? (Esther 4:13-14)

Mordecai wanted to make sure she understood the gravity of her mission. He also wanted her to know that if she wasn't willing to let her position be used for the purposes of God, that not only would Jehovah select someone else to do it, but also *"thou and thy father's house shall be destroyed."*

That is the level of commitment and dependence God has on the value of the life of an intercessor. God will choose you and give you the assignment to be the mediator for your family, your city, your church, your nation, a particular situation or whatever He decides. Once you commit to the assignment, He will open doors, persuade the heart of kings, silence the voice of the accuser and do whatever it takes to position you to execute the assignment. Just the fact that He entrusted you with the mission is assurance that as long as you obey His Voice, you cannot fail. This is the assurance we have when we will walk in the Dominion Mandate – that as long as we move by His Spirit and obey His Voice, we cannot fail. We cannot fail, because God cannot fail.

This is where blessed people often miss it – when they rely on their own strength or look at their perceived weakness. In all things, we must acknowledge God. Mordecai basically told Esther, don't think your blessing is for you alone to enjoy. Who knows, you may have only received this blessing for "such a time as this."

Sometimes the Lord will tell me to use someone for a particular assignment. He will instruct me to observe the person and watch his or her level of faithfulness and sacrifice. He will have me give them different tasks before asking them to do the great work He has for them. I understand God wants to use them and even needs to use them.

But, as a father, I also understand their need to build character to be trusted with certain assignments. Beloved, with almost 40 years in ministry, I have witnessed the enemy destroy people who have received a great anointing from God. They may have the ability to accomplish great things and damage the kingdom of hell. But, scripture admonishes us to be clothed in the whole armor of God so that we can destroy the wiles of the devil. An anointing without character is a pending disaster. It is the trusted weapon of the enemy to wait until their elevation to expose whatever character weakness has gone unchecked. He will use it to cause them to fail and betray others in the very assignment they were destined to succeed.

Samson betrayed a whole nation to lay his head in the lap of Delilah. But, the issue didn't start when he laid his head down that day. The character flaw that led him to that couch went unchecked for years. His anointing was so powerful he used the jawbone of a donkey to slay 1,000 Philistines. But, while he was anointed to destroy armies, his strength was destroyed by the whisper of a woman.

When you don't develop character to match your anointing, God cannot use you and you are subject to betray those you were assigned to help. What is recognized as your strength can be the very source of your undoing. Many great men and women of God have died prematurely because the enemy used this weapon against them.

When you decide that your own life is more important than what He has given you to do, God cannot trust you to complete your assignment. An intercessor must be trusted by God to execute His command and when you operate independently of God, you have abdicated your position in intercession, lost your usefulness and even exposed your whole family to destruction.

God is subject to His Word. He will not violate His own law. He requires a body in the Earth to execute every assignment He has on the Earth. God will work with an intercessor.

> *Wherefore when he cometh into the world, he saith, Sacrifice and offering thou wouldest not, but a body hast thou prepared me.*
> *(Hebrews 10:5)*

It is in intercession and prayer that we submit our bodies to receive the instructions of the Lord and for Him to execute His plans in the earth. This is why Apostle Paul admonished the church in Rome with the following words:

> *I beseech you therefore, brethren, by the mercies of God, that ye present your bodies a living sacrifice, holy, acceptable unto God, which is your reasonable service. And be not conformed to this world: but be ye transformed by the renewing of your mind, that ye may prove what is that good, and acceptable, and perfect, will of God.*
> *(Romans 12:1-2)*

Our ability to prove whatever God is saying is not based on who He is. He cannot fail and whatever He does will stand.

Our prayers are answered and our ability to prove His good, acceptable and perfect will is based on our availability to be a living sacrifice. We must renew our minds and not be conformed to the world. We must be willing to let God live through us. That is what was required of Esther if she was going to be used to stand in the gap for Israel. Once she understood this, she accepted the assignment and the Father gave her a Divine Key.

[15] Then Esther bade them return Mordecai this answer,

[16] Go, gather together all the Jews that are present in Shushan, and fast ye for me, and neither eat nor drink three days, night or day: I also and my maidens will fast likewise; and so will I go in unto the king, which is not according to the law: and if I perish, I perish.

[17] So Mordecai went his way, and did according to all that Esther had commanded him. (Esther 4:15-17)

Many people would like to quote the Scripture portion that says, *"and if I perish, I perish."* But, only those who are willing to fast, pray and make selfless sacrifices for a cause greater than themselves can truly satisfy what that Scripture requires.

The plot of Haman against the Jewish people was an evil plot. This was a desperate time for God's people. An enemy had risen up who was determined to annihilate them and destroy the plans and purposes of God.

[8] And Haman said unto king Ahasuerus, There is a certain people scattered abroad and dispersed among the people in all the provinces of thy kingdom; and their laws are diverse from all people; neither

keep they the king's laws: therefore it is not for the king's profit to suffer them.

⁹ If it please the king, let it be written that they may be destroyed: and I will pay ten thousand talents of silver to the hands of those that have the charge of the business, to bring it into the king's treasuries.

¹⁰ And the king took his ring from his hand, and gave it unto Haman the son of Hammed that the Agagite, the Jews' enemy.

¹¹ And the king said unto Haman, The silver is given to thee, the people also, to do with them as it seemeth good to thee.

¹² Then were the king's scribes called on the thirteenth day of the first month, and there was written according to all that Haman had commanded unto the king's lieutenants, and to the governors that were over every province, and to the rulers of every people of every province according to the writing thereof, and to every people after their language; in the name of king Ahasuerus was it written, and sealed with the king's ring.

¹³ And the letters were sent by posts into all the king's provinces, to destroy, to kill, and to cause to perish, all Jews, both young and old, little children and women, in one day, even upon the thirteenth day of the twelfth month, which is the month Adar, and to take the spoil of them for a prey.

¹⁴ The copy of the writing for a commandment to be given in every province was published unto all people, that they should be ready against that day. (Esther 3:8- 14)

It is important for you to understand that there are different dimensions to the warfare of God's people as revealed in the story of Esther and therefore the various kinds of prayer that were required to overthrow the plot of the enemy had to be very intense.

The enemy had a plan for the Jews that was very specific. In verse 13 it says:

"And the letters were sent by posts into all the king's provinces, to destroy, to kill, and to cause to perish, all Jews, both young and old, little children and women, in one day, even upon the thirteenth day of the twelfth month, which is the month Adar, and to take the spoil of them for a prey."

This is a very specific plan for a very specific group of people and suggests that this enemy intends to be relentless until he has wiped them out. Haman was not just enraged with Mordecai for not bowing down to him. Haman has escalated the battle and was being pushed by an evil force greater than the argument between two men. He didn't target just Mordecai, he went after a whole nation to destroy them in one day in order to acquire their possessions upon their demise.

This is the wickedness of the wicked. Haman didn't just wake up one day and decide to annihilate the Jews. This battle was generational warfare using a satanic altar to release spiritual wickedness and there was a power greater than Haman working behind the scenes.

You have to understand that Haman did not just rise up and go before the king to demand for the lives of God's people. He did a number of things behind the scenes and in the shadows to execute his wicked assignment. Haman was a certain type and kind of dangerous enemy that in effect caused the warfare to require the deployment of supernatural keys to obtain a supernatural deliverance.

The background of this generational battle began when Israel came out of Egypt on their way to their promised land when Amalek came out against them and began to attack them. It took the lifting up of Moses' hands assisted by Aaron and Hur on top of the mountain and Joshua fighting in the valley to defeat Amalek. This act was a demonstration of Moses' high priestly anointing backing the warfare strategies of an army that was depending on God to give them victory. But, Moses didn't gain the victory through God by lifting up his hands by himself. It took the persistent, relentless corporate prayers of Moses, Aaron and Hur *combined* to secure the battle. It was in the midst of that battle that God said from generation to generation, he would war with Amalek.

⁸ Then came Amalek, and fought with Israel in Rephidim.

⁹ And Moses said unto Joshua, Choose us out men, and go out, fight with Amalek: tomorrow I will stand on the top of the hill with the rod of God in mine hand.

¹⁰ So Joshua did as Moses had said to him, and fought with Amalek: and Moses, Aaron, and Hur went up to the top of the hill.

¹¹ And it came to pass, when Moses held up his hand, that Israel prevailed: and when he let down his hand, Amalek prevailed.

¹² But Moses' hands were heavy; and they took a stone, and put it under him, and he sat thereon; and Aaron and Hur stayed up his

hands, the one on the one side, and the other on the other side; and his hands were steady until the going down of the sun.

¹³ And Joshua discomfited Amalek and his people with the edge of the sword.

¹⁴ And the Lord said unto Moses, Write this for a memorial in a book, and rehearse it in the ears of Joshua: for I will utterly put out the remembrance of Amalek from under heaven.

¹⁵ And Moses built an altar, and called the name of it Jehovah-nissi:

¹⁶ For he said, because the Lord hath sworn that the Lord will have war with Amalek from generation to generation. (Exodus 17:8-16)

The battle was a generational battle. It just didn't show up in the days of Esther, neither did it just show up in the days of Saul. There was a strong generational undertone to the battle that was confronting the people of God, which required particular dimensions of prayer to overthrow the activities of the enemy.

This is how generational curses operate. The enemy operates from one generation to another with the aim to afflict, torment, harass and destroy the people of God.

Verses 14 and 15 say, "And the Lord said unto Moses, Write this for a memorial in a book, and rehearse it in the ears of Joshua: for I will utterly put out the remembrance of Amalek from under heaven. And Moses built an altar, and called the name of it Jehovah-nissi."

Here we see God setting up a righteous altar of remembrance. The devil is a counterfeiter. He also has satanic altars of remembrance. Satanic altars enforce these generational curses by locating a person who is willing to execute "the handwriting and ordinances that are against us" to effect the punishment associated with such altars.

Beloved, I guarantee that some of the battles you are fighting today have generational undercurrents and that is why new levels of prayer are required to overcome the enemy. But, there is power in prayer. You can release the efficacy of the Blood of Jesus and the superior sacrifice to destroy and overturn such altars. The Bible says:

Blotting out the handwriting of ordinances that was against us, which was contrary to us, and took it out of the way, nailing it to his cross; and having spoiled principalities and powers, he made a shew of them openly, triumphing over them in it. (Colossians 2:14)

When you are dealing with this kind of enemy, you will need to pray and you will need to tap into the mind of God and deploy strategy. When you are fighting new battles, you must be ready for God to give you new weapons. Haman had decided to be used by the devil to execute this wicked generational curse against the Jews. He wasn't chosen by accident. Haman was selected for this assignment by the powers of darkness.

Haman is known as the Agagatite because he was a descendant of Agag, the king of Amalek. God had instructed Saul, the first king of Israel, to kill Agag during the first battle of his reign. In his disobedience, King Saul spared Agag, the king of the Amalakites. You must remember that

God had decided that He was going to have generational warfare with Amalek.

¹ Samuel also said unto Saul, The Lord sent me to anoint thee to be king over his people, over Israel: now therefore hearken thou unto the voice of the words of the Lord.

² Thus saith the Lord of hosts, I remember that which Amalek did to Israel, how he laid wait for him in the way, when he came up from Egypt.

³ Now go and smite Amalek, and utterly destroy all that they have, and spare them not; but slay both man and woman, infant and suckling, ox and sheep, camel and ass.

⁸ And he took Agag the king of the Amalekites alive, and utterly destroyed all the people with the edge of the sword.

9 But Saul and the people spared Agag, and the best of the sheep, and of the oxen, and of the fatlings, and the lambs, and all that was good, and would not utterly destroy them: but everything that was vile and refuse, that they destroyed utterly. (1 Samuel 15:1-3; 8-9)

This Agag who was spared by Saul and the people of God was the ancestor of Haman. The Scriptures clearly reveal the origin of this battle from Amalek to Agag and from Agag to Haman. The same way Esther was chosen by God for this assignment, Haman was chosen by Satan for his assignment. God needs someone who is submitted to Him to execute his good plan for mankind. Satan needs someone who is submitted to him to execute his wicked plan. God has already planned the end from the beginning and the Bible says:

Then said I, Lo, I come (in the volume of the book it is written of me,) to do thy will, O God. (Hebrews 10:7)

When God wants to do something *for* mankind, He looks for a person who will submit to him. When Satan wants to do something *against* mankind, he locates a person who will submit to him. When we fail to pray and discover God's plan for our lives, we leave ourselves open to become a tool and weapon in the hand of the enemy to be used against the Kingdom of God. We need daily prayer for daily victory.

An intercessor must obey God and be led by His Spirit. It is in times of prophetic intercession and spiritual warfare that God will use mere men to enforce the judgment written on the wicked. This is because He alone knows that it is only the destruction of the wicked in the present that will prevent the sudden calamity that seeks to overtake the righteous in the future. Too often we think only of our present condition and forget to travail for generations yet unborn to have prevailing power. In Psalm 72:10, 15 David prayed these prophetic prayers to enforce Solomon's future:

The kings of Tarshish and of the isles shall bring presents: the kings of Sheba and Seba shall offer gifts…. And he shall live, and to him shall be given of the gold of Sheba: prayer also shall be made for him continually; and daily shall he be praised.

Those prayers came to pass in 1 Kings, Chapter 10. The Queen of Sheba came and she performed all that David had already prophesied in his prayer for Solomon. She prayed for him in verse 9 and verse 10 says:

And she gave the king an hundred and twenty talents of gold, and of spices very great store, and precious stones: there came no more such abundance of spices as these which the queen of Sheba gave to king Solomon.

David secured Solomon's prophetic destiny in prayer. It is through prophetic prayers we are made sensitive to the voice of God and block out human reasoning, which can desensitize us to His Voice and the commands and dictates of His Spirit that are only heard in times of deep intercession. This is what happened in the days of Esther. By corporate prayer, the future projected by the enemy was averted and one man's plan to destroy the future generation of a nation was dismantled.

The battle between Haman and God's people in the days of Esther had a serious history. It was a generational battle. However, Haman wasn't just operating on his own and using his earthly position to fight the Jews. He was willing to take the battle to another level.

Haman wasn't just a natural enemy; he let himself be used as a spiritual enemy by using another source of power. Haman operated in the occult and practiced different dimensions of witchcraft.

"In the first month, that is, the month Nisan, in the twelfth year of king Ahasuerus, they cast Pur, that is, the lot, before Haman from day to day, and from month to month, to the twelfth month, that is, the month Adar." (Esther 3:7)

Witchcraft involves the manipulation of satanic power for selfish goals. Haman practiced a dimension of witchcraft that included divination, casting lots, consulting the oracles, manipulation and control. Initially, he tried to control Mordecai. When that didn't work, he manipulated the king to execute a written decree against the Jews. He was very deep in occultist practices and consulted the oracles of Satan for a full year month after month. He went regularly and consistently to enforce his plan. Haman was a wicked man who was determined not to use his own power alone or his limited capability to carry out his plan. He was depending on an evil supernatural power for influence and authority to carry out his evil agenda as an agent of darkness. Haman was consistent in his occult practices for an entire year. He did it from day to day and from month to month until, through consultation with the oracles, he chose a day he could finally complete his wicked agenda.

This is why we must pray for those in authority to block satanic agendas and to restrict access to them from satanic agents. Evil will never be satisfied until it destroys good.

When Mordecai discovered the evil plot of Haman and informed Esther about the plan of their enemy, they were dealing with both a generational and spiritual battle. It was a life-threatening situation. An entire generation of God's people was about to be wiped out and so the kind of prayer that was required to overrule the activities of the enemy had to be very intense. The magnitude of the prayer was great.

Once Esther accepted her assignment, God gave her the battle strategy. This is Esther exercising the Dominion Mandate to reveal the plans of God for the people of God:

Go, gather together all the Jews that are present in Shushan, and fast ye for me, and neither eat nor drink three days, night or day: I also and my maidens will fast likewise; and so will I go in unto the king, which is not according to the law: and if I perish, I perish. (Esther 4:16)

Esther deployed a spiritual weapon that moves the hand of God. She deployed the weapons of fasting and prayer. She instructed Mordecai to proclaim a fast among the Jews. She did not depend on her own little prayer. Neither did she depend on the prayers of a few friends.

She requested the corporate prayers of all the people of God in the city. She also demanded that a dry fast for three days and nights. . This means they didn't eat nor drink anything for three days and three nights.

Fasting and prayer is one of the most intensive spiritual activities that move the hand of God into situations and circumstances. When people begin to fast and pray, they activate the supernatural power of God. When this occurs, the impossible becomes possible and there is a divine intervention.

Many times in the Scriptures, you will find God's people deploying this mighty weapon of fasting and prayer. When the weapons of fasting and prayer are deployed there are a few things that happen:

- Heaven's attention is attracted
- Heaven responds by sending an Angel
- Divine and prophetic directions are released
- Captivity is supernaturally turned around
- The impossible is made possible

When Esther and the people of God began to fast and pray, there was a divine intervention. God began to give Esther prophetic directions regarding the situation. She had a supernatural boldness to request the king's attention, which was against the law at the time. But because of the power of fasting and prayer, Esther had favor with the king. He stretched out his scepter and invited her, which was against the law.

¹ Now it came to pass on the third day, that Esther put on her royal apparel, and stood in the inner court of the king's house, over against the king's house: and the king sat upon his royal throne in the royal house, over against the gate of the house.

² And it was so, when the king saw Esther the queen standing in the court, that she obtained favour in his sight: and the king held out to Esther the golden sceptre that was in his hand. So Esther drew near, and touched the top of the sceptre.

³ Then said the king unto her, What wilt thou, queen Esther? and what is thy request? it shall be even given thee to the half of the kingdom. (Esther 5:1-3)

The fasting and prayers of Esther and the Jewish people had started to turn things around. Supernatural favor was released towards Esther.

Favor is very important for you to advance in any sphere of life and in the midst of the battles of life you will need favor. Favor causes you to receive what you do not deserve. It is out of favor that you have the words *favorite* and *favoritism*. When you obtain favor from God, you become His favorite and He demonstrates favoritism towards you. Under those circumstances you obtain what others are not able to obtain. He turns situations around and gives you a divine advantage.

One of the ways that supernatural favor is activated in difficult times is through the weapons of fasting and prayer. The king told Esther that regardless of what her request was, he was going to give her half of his kingdom.

If the power of God can be activated through fasting and prayer to move a king to grant requests, that should be an indication that God Himself will grant the requests of His people who cry out to Him day and night. There is no request too great for God to grant. It doesn't matter how long the situation has existed, God is still able to intervene.

After a series of meetings and events between the King, Esther and Haman, the Jews' enemy, the wicked plot was overruled. At the end of the story, Mordecai was honored and Haman was hanged. It took intensive fasting and prayer to overrule the plot of the enemy, but the Jews were delivered from the hands of their enemies.

So they hanged Haman and his whole family on the gallows that he had prepared for Mordecai. The very plan of Haman was to *"destroy, to kill, and to cause to perish, all Jews, both young and old, little children and women, in one day, even upon the thirteenth day of the twelfth month, which is the month Adar, and to take the spoil of them for a prey."* But, in the end Haman received the words of his mouth and even all his possessions became the possession of Mordecai:

¹ On that day did the king Ahasuerus give the house of Haman the Jews' enemy unto Esther the queen. And Mordecai came before the king; for Esther had told what he was unto her.

² And the king took off his ring, which he had taken from Haman, and gave it unto Mordecai. And Esther set Mordecai over the house of Haman. (Esther 8:1-2)

Not only did God deliver them, but He also caused the desires of their enemy to be overturned and the pit Haman dug for the righteous became a pit prepared for him. There is power in prayer. Psalm 140:6-10 (TLB) says that David prayed:

"O Jehovah, my Lord and Savior, my God and my shield—hear me as I pray! Don't let these wicked men succeed; don't let them prosper and be proud. Let their plots boomerang! Let them be destroyed by the very evil they have planned for me. Let burning coals fall down upon their heads, or throw them into the fire or into deep pits from which they can't escape."

There is great power in prayer alone. But, when the enemy escalates the battle, we must deploy additional weapons to ensure our victory. The power of fasting and prayer prevailed against a battle that was both generational and spiritual.

You may be engaged in a very difficult battle that may be life threatening and the circumstances may be beyond your control, but the power of God through the activities of fasting and prayer can overrule the activities of the enemy.

As you study the Scriptures critically, you will realize that whenever the people of God called upon God in the midst of fasting and prayer there was always a divine intervention that brought amazing results. It is time for you to deploy the supernatural power of God that can be activated through fasting and prayer into different dimensions of your life and God will give you total victory.

Satan is a counterfeiter. He will always use our ignorance to engage the trusted weapons of God against us. Not only does he depend on our ignorance of the Scriptures but also one of his trusted weapons against the Church today is our prayerlessness and our lack of knowledge concerning the Dominion Mandate. When we won't fast and pray, those whom he deploys against us will fast and pray. Other religions that seek to destroy the righteous will fast and pray to gain an advantage over us. Consider Acts 23:11-14:

"[11] But the following night the Lord stood by him and said, "Be of good cheer, Paul; for as you have testified for Me in Jerusalem, so you must also bear witness at Rome."

Paul travailed in prayer and the Lord spoke to him a promise to deliver him safe to his next assignment. But the enemy had another plan.

"¹² And when it was day, some of the Jews banded together and bound themselves under an oath, saying that they would neither eat nor drink till they had killed Paul.

¹³ Now there were more than forty who had formed this conspiracy.

¹⁴ They came to the chief priests and elders, and said, "We have bound ourselves under a great oath that we will eat nothing until we have killed Paul."

The enemy knows how to get others to work the principles against us. Even in the face of prophecy, the enemy will still work against us. But, the same way the enemy uses satanic agents to subvert our course; the Lord knows how to deploy the righteous to enforce His promises when we are operating in our assignment and vigilant in our prayers. In Acts 23:20-24 the satanic plot was averted.

"And he said, "The Jews have agreed to ask that you bring Paul down to the council tomorrow, as though they were going to inquire more fully about him. But do not yield to them, for more than forty of them lie in wait for him, men who have bound themselves by an oath that they will neither eat nor drink till they have killed him; and now they are ready, waiting for the promise from you."

So the commander let the young man depart, and commanded him, "Tell no one that you have revealed these things to me."

And he called for two centurions, saying, "Prepare two hundred soldiers, seventy horsemen, and two hundred spearmen to go to Caesarea at the third hour of the night; and provide mounts to set Paul on, and bring him safely to Felix the governor."

The same way Satan used the bodies of 40 men to try and kill Paul through fasting and prayer, God deployed the body of

Paul's nephew to reveal and avert the satanic plot. May your prayers and fasting deliver you and deploy others to speak on your behalf in the corridors of power. Prayer moves God!

The fasting and prayers of Esther and the Jews released supernatural favor that brought about a mighty deliverance. It is time for a mighty deliverance for you and your loved ones. I prophesy and declare upon you and your loved ones new seasons of favor and divine interventions. The hand of the Lord supernaturally lift you to where you belong and grant you the desires of your heart!

In 2014, a vicious, deadly virus known as Ebola attacked the West African Sub-region. Citizens in most of the countries surrounding Ghana were attacked by this deadly disease and many lost their lives. Around the world, news outlets predicted that Ghana was next in line to be attacked.

I led the church in praying fervently to build a hedge around the nation and to repel this deadly disease from Ghana since it would have brought untold hardship to the already suffering masses of our people. We called for national prayer and fasting and we sought Divine immunity from Elohim. Amazingly, in answer to our prayer and that of many others, the Lord prevented this deadly virus from attacking our people.

There were predictions that the virus would have become a pandemic by the Year 2015 and international mobilization and legislation was put in place and was under discussion to restrict travel to the region, which would have greatly disadvantaged people who were already struggling with abject poverty. Indeed, there was a move to quarantine West Africans and to limit travellers coming from the western nations. I called for 24-hour prayer and fasting repeatedly to avert this legislation and overrule the agenda of Satan to afflict and torment the West African nations and to control our gates and borders. We cried out to the Lord day and night and the judgment of men was overruled by the prayers of those who were willing to remain on their knees and stand in the gap to enforce God's agenda for the West African nations.

Beloved, we cannot just rest on our laurels and believe that God is in control of this world and He's just going to work it all out. When God gives us the burden to pray, we must travail until the burden is lifted. Scripture says –

"For as soon as Zion travailed, she brought forth her children. "Shall I bring to the birth and not cause to bring forth?" saith the LORD." (Isaiah 66:8)

There is great satisfaction in knowing that when we pray, God answers and situations of trouble and hardship are averted.

He shall see of the travail of his soul, and shall be satisfied: by his knowledge shall my righteous servant justify many; for he shall bear their iniquities. (Isaiah 53:11)

Chapter Summary:

- The providence of God has placed each of us in a unique position in the Earth. It is from this position, if we will exercise the Dominion Mandate, we will be able to bring God's counsel into the affairs of men.

- We must not consider the anointing alone on our lives. We must work to build and develop character so that we will be able to complete our mission.

- God wants to use you and every gift He has placed in you. Can He trust you to submit to Him when He needs to use what He has given you?

- Many of the prolonged battles of our lives are both generational and spiritual. We can be dealing with family altars that repeat curses generation after generation. We can also be dealing with challenges from the occult practices of our enemy. We must pray for God to reveal the nature of the battle so that we use the associated weapons of our warfare. We must never be ignorant of the devices of Satan.

- We must remember to pray for generations yet unborn to enforce their victories now. Prayers live on after we have left the Earth.

- Fasting and prayer is one of the most intensive spiritual activities that move the hand of God into situations and circumstances.

Chapter 8

The Prayers of Daniel

"No one can believe how powerful prayer is and what it can effect, except those who have learned it by experience. Whenever I have prayed earnestly, I have been heard and have obtained more than I prayed for. God sometimes delays, but He always comes." — ***Martin Luther***

In the previous chapter we saw how Esther was divinely positioned by God to exercise the Dominion Mandate in prayer and gain favor with King Ahasuerus through the weapons of fasting and prayer. By taking authority through corporate intercession, the people of God were divinely enabled to destroy the evil plot of the wicked and execute the judgments of Elohim in both a spiritual and a generational battle. The weapons of our warfare are mighty through God to the pulling down of strongholds, but we must be willing to exercise our Dominion Mandate by inviting God to get involved in the affairs of the Earth.

In this chapter you are going to realize the power of prayer and how far it travels when we exercise the Dominion Mandate from any position we find ourselves in on the Earth. In the last chapter we examined how God placed Esther in a position of worldly blessing and honor in order for her to use her Dominion Mandate and bring God on the scene from her position as queen. In this chapter, we will see Daniel, who is a slave in a foreign kingdom – but his position in the Earth is what makes him a mighty weapon in the hand of Elohim. Because he was willing to walk in the power of his Dominion

Mandate in spite of his earthly position, God used him to reveal the powers behind the scenes and to cause angels to come in response to his prayers.

It is the prayers of Daniel that brought into manifestation the prophecy of Jeremiah the prophet concerning the end of the captivity of God's people. Jeremiah prophesied that the captivity of God's people was going to last seventy years and it took the strong persistent prayers of Daniel to overthrow the satanic embargo in the Heavenlies through angelic intervention and reinforcement. You are about to encounter the life of one that believed in prayer and saw a manifestation of answered prayers.

The prophecy of Jeremiah was recorded and kept in the scrolls in the temple and at the appointed time Daniel began to study the scrolls and found out that the captivity of God's people was supposed to last seventy years and the time had come for their deliverance. The prophecy is found in Jeremiah 29:10:

"For thus saith the Lord, That after seventy years be accomplished at Babylon I will visit you, and perform my good word toward you, in causing you to return to this place."

But, the prophecy was conditional. Daniel saw that the time was finished and the promise was not fulfilled. There was a clause written in Jeremiah 29:11-12 that needed to be met before there would be a manifestation:

"For I know the thoughts that I think toward you, saith the Lord, thoughts of peace, and not of evil, to give you an expected end. Then

shall ye call upon me, and ye shall go and pray unto me, and I will hearken unto you."

The prophecy expressly said that God would hear their prayers. But, that wouldn't be the solution to break their captivity. He wanted them to prepare themselves through prayer before there was to be a release from captivity. It wasn't going to be easy. They would have to seek the Lord with all their heart.

And ye shall seek me, and find me, when ye shall search for me with all your heart. And I will be found of you, saith the Lord: and I will turn away your captivity, and I will gather you from all the nations, and from all the places whither I have driven you, saith the Lord; and I will bring you again into the place whence I caused you to be carried away captive. (Jeremiah 29:10-14)

Daniel was a student of prophecy and that gave him the ability to embrace the right spiritual posture that began the process of deliverance for God's people. In Daniel chapter 9, Daniel begins to pray a very long prayer of supplication and repentance. He does not just repent for his own sins, but he confesses and takes ownership for the sins of the nation. This is the prayer of an intercessor.

The prayer of supplication and repentance becomes a stirring lamentation and shows us the activity of a true intercessor. He aligns himself with the transgressor and owns up to the iniquity that led to captivity.

"Therefore will I divide him a portion with the great, and he shall divide the spoil with the strong; because he hath poured out his soul unto

death: and he was numbered with the transgressors; and he bare the sin of many, and made intercession for the transgressors." (Isaiah 53:12)

The scripture in Isaiah is a prophecy about Jesus. But, it shows us that intercession – especially for transgression – is a travailing prayer. *"He poured out his soul unto death."* There is labor in prayer. The prayer of intercession is an agonizing prayer. This is the kind of prayer that moves God. Daniel is not asking God to bless him and make him the Prime Minister. He doesn't request that God forgive him alone because he didn't do anything to deserve his current state. There is nothing wrong with asking God to bless you. But, the prayer that was going to release the nation from captivity was going to require travail and labor – deep intercession. Daniel's persistent prayers released angelic assistance.

"And whiles I was speaking, and praying, and confessing my sin and the sin of my people Israel, and presenting my supplication before the Lord my God for the holy mountain of my God; Yea, whiles I was speaking in prayer, even the man Gabriel, whom I had seen in the vision at the beginning, being caused to fly swiftly, touched me about the time of the evening oblation."
(Daniel 9:20-21)

The book of Daniel gives us insight into the spiritual realm and it shows us what happens when God's people exercise the Dominion Mandate. It also gives a clear revelation of angelic activity in response to the prayers of God's people. Your prayers have tremendous power to move angels into flight.

Daniel also deployed the weapons of fasting and prayer that Esther had deployed. He was in a three-week period of fasting and prayer like Elijah. When ordinary men and women use the Dominion Mandate and enter into fasting and prayer they are able to become extraordinary weapons in the Hand of Elohim. The scriptures clearly reveal that from the first day that Daniel began to pray he received Heavens' attention and an angel was sent in response to his prayers.

It is important for you to understand that the moment you begin to pray you get Heavens' attention and God responds by sending an angel! The reason for the delays in the answers to prayer is the satanic resistance in the heavens. Strong, persistent prayers activate angelic ministry that has the capacity to destroy every satanic resistance in the Heavens.

The prince of the kingdom of Persia who was the spiritual ruler over the Persian kingdom where God's people were in captivity had formed a barricade that resisted the angel that was bringing the answer to Daniel's prayers. It is important for you to understand that besides the physical king that ruled over the Persian kingdom, there was a spiritual kingdom governed by Satan's representative who had the assignment to ensure that the agenda for that territory or domain was carried out.

There is a spiritual kingdom – the Kingdom of God – and we as God's people are at war against Satan's kingdom – the Kingdom of Darkness – which is also spiritual.

"For we wrestle not against flesh and blood, but against principalities, against powers, against the rulers of the darkness of

this world, against spiritual wickedness in high places." (Ephesians 6:12)

Prayer is a spiritual exercise and the warfare is spiritual and it is with a spiritual enemy.

"For though we walk in the flesh, we do not war after the flesh: (For the weapons of our warfare are not carnal, but mighty through God to the pulling down of strong holds;) Casting down imaginations, and every high thing that exalteth itself against the knowledge of God, and bringing into captivity every thought to the obedience of Christ." (2 Corinthians 10:3-5)

We don't war against flesh and blood, but beloved, we do war! If we don't fight the good fight of faith we cannot win. We must understand that we have some powerful weapons that are mighty through God – to pull down the strong holds – the satanic barriers and wicked resistance of the enemy. It is through the exercise of prayer and fasting that we deploy the trusted, mighty powerful weapons of God.

Daniel was using the powerful spiritual weapons of fasting and prayer that destroyed the resistance of the enemy. It took twenty-one days to receive the relevant angelic assistance for the angel that was bringing the answer to Daniel's prayer to break through the satanic resistance.

It is important for you to realize that the moment you begin to pray, God answers and responds to your prayers by sending an angel. What causes the delays in the answer to your prayer is the satanic resistance in the heavens. That is why you cannot quit. You must destroy imaginations, every high thing that is against the knowledge of God and bring thoughts into captivity to the obedience of Christ. We cannot live anyway, anyhow, and obey the dictates of the flesh if we are going to prevail over the enemy in prayer.

Daniel didn't just pray. He fasted. He didn't just pray and fast – he confessed God before men and let it be known that he was not going to conform to the customs and traditions of the nation where he found himself.

No matter where you are located in the seven continents of Earth, you must not abdicate your Kingdom citizenship. Psalm 2 declares:

Ask of Me, and I will give You The nations for Your inheritance, and the ends of the earth for Your possession. **You shall break them with a rod of iron; You shall dash them to pieces like a potter's vessel.**

It is the Church that has this Covenant Promise. This is the power we have through Christ. To ask in prayer for every inheritance related to Christ and His Kingdom. Pray "Thy Kingdom Come!" When we pray we enforce and superimpose His Kingdom and His Will over the plan of the enemy. We have this authority through Christ to use the rod of iron – the judgment written – and dash the kingdoms of darkness to pieces as we superimpose the Kingdom of God and overrule the agenda of Satan.

Today, many of God's children are discouraged because of unanswered prayers but the revelation of the spirit world in the book of Daniel gives clear insight about how enemy forces intercept and block the answer to the prayers of God's people. If Daniel had stopped praying on the tenth or twentieth day, his angel may not have been able to come through with his answer. He had to persist in prayer.

Today, I want you to know that God still answers prayer. Discouragement, unbelief and doubt are some of the major weapons the enemy uses to hinder the answers to your prayers. His main agenda is to discredit God's Word. So he sets up and orchestrates a resistance when people pray. He is the "father of lies" and he will use the tool of deception to make sure you encounter restrictions and barriers when you exercise the keys of prayer, fasting and especially when you give.

Those three trusted weapons invade his territory. They involve sacrifice. He understands the power of sacrifice and he wants to silence you, desensitize you and take away your self-confidence and convince you that your prayers aren't working.

When you use this three-fold weapon (prayer, fasting and giving) it will cause demonic reactions. As soon as believers see the reactions, they back off. They quit or get very discouraged. They assume this will make Satan leave them alone. But, instead the battle intensifies and the warfare increases to make them stop and make them passive toward the enemy while he remains aggressive and violent toward them. In fact, now that the battle has commenced, if we back off, he moves in and takes over. The key here is to not grow weary and don't faint. The scripture tells us:

And let us not be weary in well doing: for in due season we shall reap, if we faint not. (Galatians 6:9)

And he spake a parable unto them to this end, that men ought always to pray, and not to faint. (Luke 18:1)

Persistence breaks resistance. You cannot give up. You must remain vigilant and purposeful in prayer. It took twenty-one days of consistent prayers for Daniel's angel to receive the needed assistance to destroy the resistance of the enemy. Michael who is an Archangel came to break the resistance of the prince of Persia for the deliverance of God's people to begin.

Jeremiah's prophecy was true and God wanted to accomplish His Word. But, even though it was time for the manifestation of the prophetic word, it was not going to happen automatically. Someone had to fulfill the rules of engagement, exercise the Dominion Mandate and enter into the realm of intercession to cause the word of the Lord to come to pass. You must war, using the prophecy, to engage the enemy. Paul charged Timothy to war a good warfare according to the prophecies that had already been given:

This charge I commit unto thee, son Timothy, according to the prophecies which went before on thee, that thou by them mightest war a good warfare. (1 Timothy 1:18)

Today, I want you to know that God still answers prayer. Do not allow discouragement, unbelief and doubt to deceive you. The enemy uses these as major weapons to stop you from travailing in prayer and to give up before you receive the answers to your prayers. You have to keep persisting until there is a manifestation of answered prayers. Remember the first day you begin to pray, God sends an angel. Consistent and persistent prayers increase angelic activity.

It will also come to pass that before they call, I will answer; and while they are still speaking, I will hear. (Isaiah 65:24)

It doesn't matter how long you have been in captivity, strong prayers can break the bondage of the enemy and bring you deliverance. Daniel was a man of consistent prayers. He prayed three times a day and that provoked his enemies to cause the king to pass a law against prayer. In spite of the law, Daniel maintained his prayer life and this provoked the enemy more.

Now when Daniel knew that the writing was signed, he went into his house; and his windows being open in his chamber toward Jerusalem, he kneeled upon his knees three times a day, and prayed, and gave thanks before his God, as he did aforetimes. (Daniel 6:10)

Daniel was thrown into the lion's den because he did not comply with the king's decree. The next day when the king came to check on the state of Daniel, this is the statement he made in Daniel 6:19-22:

[19] Then the king arose very early in the morning, and went in haste unto the den of lions.

[20] And when he came to the den, he cried with a lamentable voice unto Daniel: and the king spake and said to Daniel, O Daniel, servant of the living God, is thy God, whom thou servest continually, able to deliver thee from the lions?

[21] Then said Daniel unto the king, O king, live forever.

²² My God hath sent his angel, and hath shut the lions' mouths, that they have not hurt me: forasmuch as before him innocency was found in me; and also before thee, O king, have I done no hurt.

The prayers of Daniel activated the ministry of angels. The angels of God shut the mouth of the lions so that they could not touch Daniel. The conspiracy of Daniel's enemies was strong and powerful but the power of prayer overruled the power of the evil conspiracies and Daniel won the victory. His enemies were thrown into the lion's den and the lions destroyed them.

Prayer does move God and you can realize from Daniel's example that there is always divine intervention for God's people when they call upon God.

Chapter Summary:

- Your position in the Earth can and will be used by God if you will exercise the Dominion Mandate and invite Him to get involved in the affairs of the Earth.

- Fasting, prayer, and corporate intercession are mighty weapons against spiritual and generational battles.

- Angels come in response to our prayers. Your prayers have power to release angelic reinforcements.

- Prophecy is conditional. God will and God can do anything. But, He must be invited through an intercessor exercising their Dominion Mandate and praying for Him to get involved.

- Intercession – especially for transgression – is labor. We must be willing to agonize in prayer and take ownership and responsibility for the target of our prayers. Great intercessors align themselves with the transgressor. This kind of prayer gets God's attention.

- We are in a spiritual battle. Our assignment is to superimpose the Kingdom of God over the Kingdom of Darkness through exercising our Dominion Mandate and praying Thy Kingdom Come.

- The three-fold weapon of giving, fasting and prayer is mighty and will bring great damage to the Kingdom of Darkness. Satan knows this, so whenever you deploy that weapon his response involves retaliation to get you to doubt God, get discouraged and discredit the Word of God. But, don't give up! It is your persistence in deploying that weapon that will break the resistance of satanic embargoes.

Chapter 9

Activating Angelic Ministry

"The Angels are the dispensers and administrators of the Divine beneficence toward us. They regard our safety, undertake our defense, direct our ways, and exercise a constant solicitude that no evil befall us." – **John Calvin**

In the preceding chapters we have seen how ordinary men and women exercised their Dominion Mandate and enforced the Kingdom of God through prayer. Prayer is the instructions by which the angels move to bring to manifestation the answer from Heaven. They move in response to the Word of God lifted by the intercessor. The intercessor through prayer activates the ministry of angels. We saw how ordinary men in the Bible – before Christ came activated the ministry of angels. Because the scripture is written through the inspiration of the Holy Spirit, we see that the prayers of men activated Angels. But, when we read the true stories of men and women who by prayer witnessed great revivals – do we really see how important and key the activation of angels was? If there is a record of the activity of angels, surely it will record greater activity in this latter age than the former. Before we can discuss the prayer life of our great intercessor and savior – the Lord Jesus Christ – we must discuss His partners in ministry, the Angels. Indeed, we must know that through our Dominion Mandate we activate the ministry of angels.

Angels can be either active or dormant in your life. Before we can have the ministry of angels working in our lives, we must first understand what it is that causes angels to be "activated." Although angels are always with us, they can remain dormant and never even begin to operate and minister for us as God intended. Angels have a specific ministry to believers.

The writer of Hebrews describes the relationship of Christ to the angels in Hebrews 1:4-7)

"Being made so much better than the angels, as he hath by inheritance obtained a more excellent name than they. For unto which of the angels said he at any time, Thou art my Son, this day have I begotten thee? And again, I will be to him a Father, and he shall be to me a Son? And again, when he bringeth in the firstbegotten into the world, he saith, And let all the angels of God worship him. And of the angels he saith, Who maketh his angels spirits, and his ministers a flame of fire." (Hebrews 1:4-7)

He sums up their existing assignment and role in the life of the believer in Hebrews 1:13-14. He says they are subject to Christ and it is their role to help those who will inherit salvation:

"But to which of the angels said he at any time, Sit on my right hand, until I make thine enemies thy footstool? Are they not all ministering spirits, sent forth to minister for them who shall be heirs of salvation."

So the angels have a ministry to serve alongside and help the saints to make the enemies of Christ become His footstool. In order to deploy this angelic assistance, we must know the Word of God and be able to use His Word to deploy the angels.

The Bible is God speaking to you and me. God said in Isaiah 55:11 that His Word will not return to Him void. In other words, when the Word of God is spoken out of the mouth of a believer, it is the same as God the Father speaking it, and the angels respond to God's Word spoken by a believer the same way they do when God Himself gives a command from His throne! We can deploy the services of angels in prayer by speaking on the authority of God's word. This is how we activate the ministry of angels to manifest our Dominion Mandate.

The angels are the mighty servants of God who constantly serve Him always doing His will. The Psalmist described their activity like this:

Bless the LORD, you His angels, Mighty in strength, who perform His word, Obeying the VOICE of His word! Bless the LORD, all you His hosts, You who serve Him, doing His will. (Psalm 103:20-21)

We understand from this verse of Scripture that angels respond to the commands of God's Word. Angels still do this today for the believer who will exercise the Dominion Mandate. God gives angels their instructions, and they listen and obey. That also means that when we say what God's Word says — when we speak God's Word — we loose or deploy angels to work on our behalf. But when we speak words contrary to what God has said, we bind or hinder our angels from working for us.

Hebrews chapter 1 verse 14 tells us: "Are not all angels ministering spirits sent forth to minister for them who will inherit salvation?" This scripture tells us that angels are spirits; therefore they are not usually seen. Just because you don't see an angel does not mean one is not there.

Angels are deployed from the presence of the Father – from the Throne Room – to minister for the heirs of salvation. We are not to serve angels, neither do angels serve humans, but we all serve God. Just as we have an earthly assignment, their assignment is to assist us in completing the mission. Jesus said this about our relationship with the angels:

I tell you, whoever acknowledges me before men, the Son of Man will also acknowledge him before the angels of God. But he who disowns me before men will be disowned before the angels of God. (Luke 12:8-9)

So the angels are watching how we believe, serve and respond to Christ in order to respond to us. They are watching our level of submission to determine how they submit to our commands.

It was the woman who was made from a man, and not the man who was made from a woman. He wasn't created for her. She was created for him. And so, because of this, and also because of the angels, a woman ought to wear something on her head, as a sign of her authority. (1 Corinthians 11:8-10)

The angels operate by order, by regime and under submission to the Godhead. They respond to and obey us as they observe that we also understand and respect that same order of authority.

The Bible says that at the end of Daniel's three weeks of fasting and praying for an answer from God, the angel Gabriel appeared to Daniel and said to him, "I have come because of your words." (Daniel 10:12)

How many angels do we have at our disposal? Jesus described the angels at His disposal:

"Do you think I cannot call on my Father, and he will at once put at my disposal more than twelve legions of angels?" Matthew 26:53

In scripture, Mount Zion represents the Church. In Hebrews Apostle Paul encourages the Church with these words:

"But you have come to Mount Zion, to the heavenly Jerusalem, the city of the living God. You have come to thousands upon thousands of angels in joyful assembly..." (Hebrews 12:22)

David tried to number the angels he saw:

"The chariots of God [another term for angel] are tens of thousands and thousands of thousands; the Lord has come from Sinai into his sanctuary." (Psalm 68:17)

The prophet attempted to describe how great the multitude was surrounding the throne of God:

"A river of fire was flowing, coming out from before Him. Thousands upon thousands attended him; ten thousand times ten thousand stood before Him. The court was seated, and the books were opened." (Daniel 7:10)

On the Isle of Patmos, Apostle John was overwhelmed as he described the angels:

Then I looked and heard the voice of many angels, numbering thousands upon thousands, and ten thousand times ten thousand. They encircled the throne and the living creatures and the elders. (Revelation 5:11)

Jesus said He had power to call on more than 12 legions of angels. It is said a legion in the Roman army was made up of 6,000 soldiers. So being able to call on 12 legions of angels meant Jesus would command an army of 72,000 angels. Ten thousand times ten thousand equals 100 million. But, in the Greek language, at the time these verses were written by the psalmist, ten thousand was the largest number you could have. So ten thousand times ten thousand was a number too big to be imagined!

Beloved, God has an unending supply of help at your disposal if you will obey His Voice, be filled with His Spirit and call on His Name. When you exercise the Dominion Mandate, God will put angels into flight to respond to His Word spoken in prayer.

So when angels hear you saying, *"Thank You, Father, no evil shall befall me nor shall any plague come near my dwelling,"* (Psalm 91:10) they will come to your aid because you are giving voice to God's Word. Even if you cannot quote the verse perfectly, they can still come to your rescue.

Psalm 91 says we can make God our dwelling place. It says, *"He who dwells in the shelter of the Most High will rest in the shadow of the Almighty. I WILL SAY OF THE LORD, `He is my refuge and my fortress, my God, in whom I trust."*

You make the Most High your dwelling the same way that David did: by SAYING OF THE LORD that He is your dwelling! Your confession that He is your refuge and fortress is what makes God become your refuge and fortress. Giving charge to His angels to bear you up and keep you from dashing your foot against a stone. The Amplified version expounds on the requirements for this level of protection:

Because you have made the Lord your refuge, and the Most High your dwelling place, there shall no evil befall you, nor any plague or calamity come near your tent. For He will give His angels [especial] charge over you to accompany and defend and preserve you in all your ways [of obedience and service]. They shall bear you up on their hands, lest you dash your foot against a stone.(Psalm 91:9-12)

And what does God do when you make the Lord your refuge and fortress? He commands His angels to guard you in all your ways so that no harm befalls you nor any disasters overtake you. Angels receive this assignment from God the Father to protect those who obey and serve Christ. They move to enforce His Word when such people confess His Word.

This is what Shadrach, Meshach and Abednego did before they were thrown into the fiery furnace. They boldly declared, *"The God we serve is able to deliver us from the burning fiery furnace, and he will deliver us out of your hand, O King!"* They stood their ground in faith. And what was the outcome? God sent an angel to keep them from burning. The angel heard God's Word coming from the lips of these courageous saints and he harkened unto their words.

Your ability to use the Word of God either binds or unleashes the angels. It is with the key of prayer that we unlock heavenly access to angelic assistance and intervention.

Prayer gives us revelation. Revelation gives us access to Heaven. Having the access gives us authority in the Earth to exercise our Dominion Mandate and release our angels. Prayer moves God! To walk in dominion on Earth, you must understand the ordinances of heaven.

Knowest thou the ordinances of heaven? canst thou set the dominion thereof in the earth? (Job 38:33)

It is significant to note that angelic activity was normal for Jesus. He knew it was needed. He expected it. There was no question about it. What level of glory Jesus must have walked in to have this heavenly activity in His life. Jesus knew the power of sacrifice (John 12:24). Jesus lived a life of sacrifice and devotion that opened the windows of heaven, releasing angels to minister with Him in the earth. What purpose would there be for angels to ascend and descend upon Jesus? They were needed to minister alongside with Jesus as He manifested heaven on earth.

Before Jesus began His earthly ministry we see Him being led by the Spirit to the wilderness in fasting and prayer for 40 days (Matthew 4:1). At the end of His temptation in the wilderness, the angels appeared to strengthen Him (Matt. 4:11).

After that, He was launched in the power of the Spirit with a continual manifestation of heaven on earth (Luke 4:14). The angels of God were bringing answers from heaven to earth. This same ministry is available to us when we pray.

God sent His angel to protect Paul and those with whom Paul was sailing as stated in Acts 27. He boarded a ship sailing to Rome and along the way a dangerous and violent storm arose. This life-threatening situation brought a lot of fear and hopelessness to everyone on board the ship. It was in the midst of this dark and bleak situation that God sent an angel to speak to Paul who conveyed the message of hope and direction.

For this very night an angel of the God to whom I belong and whom I serve stood before me, saying, 'Do not be afraid, Paul; you must stand before Caesar; and behold, God has granted you all those who are sailing with you.' Therefore, keep up your courage, men, for I believe God that it will turn out exactly as I have been told. (Acts 27:21-25)

The ship ran aground and stuck fast into a sandbar but all the men were able to reach land.

If you are the captain of an army, angels are the troops at your disposal. I encourage you to use the Dominion Mandate and activate the ministry of angels through prayer and intercession.

Angels acknowledge their role in helping us fulfill our destiny. The Bible says:

I, John, am the one who heard and saw these things. And when I had heard and seen them, I fell down to worship at the feet of the angel who had been showing them to me. But he said to me, "Do not do it! I am a fellow servant with you and with your brothers the prophets and of all who keep the words of this book. Worship God!" (Revelation 22:8-9)

If you know God's Word by heart but refuse to proclaim it, the power of His Word cannot be released. The Bible does not say that angels heed His Word. No, it says that "His angels, who excel in strength, who do His word, heeding the *voice* of His word" (Psalm 103:20-21). Give voice to God's

Word and see His angels respond. His angels are activated for your benefit when you exercise the Dominion Mandate and speak His Word!

Chapter Summary:

Here are some keys to understand the angelic ministry in this dispensation:

- When we exercise the Dominion Mandate in prayer, Angels have been given the assignment to help us manifest what we have prayed. They respond to the VOICE of His Word released in prayer. – Psalm 103:20-21
- Angels are not to be worshipped as they are fellow servants with us – Revelation 19:10 and Revelation 22:8-9
- They are distinct from human beings and higher than humans with powers far beyond our abilities in this present age – 2 Peter 2:11
- Even though they are with God and under His authority, they are subject to His commands and they do not know everything about us or His plans for us even though they do desire to know – 1 Peter 1:11-12 and Matthew 24:36
- They can be bound by God and are subject to His judgment – Jude 1:6
- We will also judge the angels – 1 Corinthians 6:3

- When God sends an angel to assist you, they have come to execute His Word. They will do what He says – Psalm 103:20

Chapter 10

The Prayers of our Lord Jesus Christ

"There is no power like that of prevailing prayer, of Abraham pleading for Sodom, Jacob wrestling in the stillness of the night, Moses standing in the breach, Hannah intoxicated with sorrow, David heartbroken with remorse and grief, Jesus in sweat of blood. Add to this list from the records of the church your personal observation and experience, and always there is the cost of passion unto blood. Such prayer prevails. It turns ordinary mortals into men of power. It brings power. It brings fire. It brings rain. It brings life. It brings God." – **Samuel Chadwick**

Jesus Christ came to teach us to enforce the Dominion Mandate by not just bringing God into situations, but indeed giving us the instruction to pray – *Thy Kingdom Come* and permitting us to access the keys to the Kingdom of Heaven that releases all of the nomenclature of the Kingdom into the Earth. Now, armed with these new weapons, we no longer just subdue and resist the Kingdom of Darkness but we have received power to overrule, overthrow and destroy the Kingdom of Darkness.

"Behold, I give unto you power to tread on serpents and scorpions, and over all the power of the enemy: and nothing shall by any means hurt you." (Luke 10:19)

It is through our prayers that we enforce the Dominion Mandate and release the efficacy of the Kingdom of God. Prayer is one of the main things that our Lord Jesus Christ engaged in. He is the living Word. There are three different manifestations of the Word. There is the spoken Word, the written Word and the Living Word. The Rhema, the Logos and the Revealed Word. The Rhema is the spoken word. We need the Rhema. Faith comes by hearing and hearing the Word. We need the Logos. Every word in scripture is profitable for our learning. But, it is in prayer that we locate and gain access to the Living Word, the Revealed Word. Jesus Christ is the Living Word.

As the Living Word, Jesus found it necessary to always be in communication with the Father in order for the purposes of God to manifest. His constant communication with the Father is prayer. Prayer is a lifestyle for our Lord Jesus Christ even today.

Wherefore he is able also to save them to the uttermost that come unto God by him, seeing he ever liveth to make intercession for them. (Hebrews 7:25)

There is nothing that Jesus Christ did without consulting with the Heavenly Father. At every important season of His life, He went into very strong prayer.

He Rose Up Early to Pray

In keeping with His lifestyle, Jesus Christ rose up long before daybreak to pray (Mark 1: 35). This empowered him to discern the will and purposes of God. He was not ready to please and follow the dictates of men but rather through prayer, He knew the will of God and fulfilled it. His attitude of rising up a great while before day gave Him a Divine Advantage over the day. This ensured that He would have advance knowledge to deal with whatever He would be facing throughout the day. He was also training the disciples to seek the Lord early.

The success of Jesus' mission was based on two things: He stayed in constant communication with the Father by prayer and He obeyed what He saw and heard in times of prayer.

> *So Jesus answered them by saying, I assure you, most solemnly I tell you, the Son is able to do nothing of Himself (of His own accord); but He is able to do only what He sees the Father doing, for whatever the Father does is what the Son does in the same way [in His turn]. I am able to do nothing from Myself [independently, of My own accord—but only as I am taught by God and as I get His orders]. Even as I hear, I judge [I decide as I am bidden to decide. As the voice comes to Me, so I give a decision], and My judgment is right (just, righteous), because I do not seek or consult My own will [I have no desire to do what is pleasing to Myself, My own aim, My own purpose] but only the will and pleasure of the Father Who sent Me. (John 5:19,30 AMP)*

Jesus was determined and focused on obedience to the Father. His success was because He did what He saw and heard from the Father in times of prayer. God taught Him and instructed Him in prayer. This was His lesson to us. This is the only way we can be successful in life. By prayer we can know and obey the will of the Father and thereby exercise our Dominion Mandate.

It is important for you as a Christian to spend time in the Word and prayer every day especially before beginning the day. This strengthens and empowers you to deal with the challenges of the day. Prayer is a daily necessity for daily triumph.

Before His Baptism He Prayed

Now when all the people were baptized, it came to pass, that Jesus also being baptized, and praying, the heaven was opened, And the Holy Ghost descended in a bodily shape like a dove upon him, and a voice came from heaven, which said, Thou art my beloved Son; in thee I am well pleased. (Luke 3:21-22)

Before His baptism by John the Baptist, our Lord Jesus Christ was praying as He approached the water. Everyone else went to be baptized, but it was not recorded that they were praying. However, Jesus Christ was praying and the scriptures declare that the heavens were opened and the Holy Spirit descended upon him and a Voice from Heaven spoke in response to His prayers. It was the prayers that caused the heavens to be opened.

The atmosphere of opened heavens is critical for divine operations and manifestations. When there is an atmosphere of open heavens, there is a close communion and fellowship with God; there is a manifestation of answered prayers; and there are divine and angelic activities.

There is a dimension in prayer that you will always come out with a note of victory. When you pray, you will know God has heard your prayer. This is why you must be consistent in prayer.

During His Forty Day Fast

When the Spirit of God came upon Him after He came out of the River Jordan, Jesus Christ was led by the Spirit, into the wilderness where He spent 40 forty days and nights in intensive fasting and prayer and returned in the power of the Holy Spirit. The scripture says in Luke 4:1-2:

And Jesus, full of the Holy Spirit, returned from the Jordan and was led by the Spirit in the wilderness for forty days, being tempted by the devil. And he ate nothing during those days. And when they were ended, he was hungry.

Beloved, even to fast and pray, Jesus never relied on Himself alone. He was full of the Holy Spirit and allowed the Holy Spirit to lead Him even into prayer. It is one thing to be full of the Spirit and it is another thing to walk in the power of the Holy Ghost. Walking in the power of the Holy Ghost was a result of the fasting, the prayer and engaging the enemy.

It is the Holy Spirit who teaches us to pray and what to pray for. This was Jesus' lifestyle and what made Him destroy the works of darkness. We are instructed likewise:

Likewise the Spirit also helpeth our infirmities: for we know not what we should pray for as we ought: but the Spirit itself maketh intercession for us with groanings which cannot be uttered. (Romans 8:26)

Even though he was the Living Word, he deployed the written Word to overcome the enemy. He overcame the enemy through prayer, fasting and the Word. After the time of intensive spiritual warfare, the angels ministered to Him.

And he was there in the wilderness forty days, tempted of Satan; and was with the wild beasts; and the angels ministered unto him. Mark 1:13

Jesus Habit of Prayer

It was the lifestyle of Christ to withdraw Himself to pray. He often went into the wilderness and spent time with the Father before He came out to minister to the people.

> *And He withdrew himself into the wilderness, and prayed. And it came to pass on a certain day, as He was teaching, that there were Pharisees and doctors of the law sitting by, which were come out of every town of Galilee, and Judaea, and Jerusalem: and the power of the Lord was present to heal them. (Luke 5:16-17)*

The times of prayer caused Him to be endued with supernatural power to preach, teach, and minister healing and deliverance. The scriptures declare that He was teaching and the power of the Lord was present to heal. The times of prayer empowered our Lord Jesus Christ to walk and operate in the supernatural.

On one occasion, He spent long periods of time praying. Then He walked on the sea.

[22] And straightway Jesus constrained his disciples to get into a ship, and to go before him unto the other side, while he sent the multitudes away.

[23] And when he had sent the multitudes away, he went up into a mountain apart to pray: and when the evening was come, he was there alone.

[24] But the ship was now in the midst of the sea, tossed with waves: for the wind was contrary.

[25] And in the fourth watch of the night Jesus went unto them, walking on the sea.

²⁶ And when the disciples saw him walking on the sea, they were troubled, saying, It is a spirit; and they cried out for fear.

²⁷ But straightway Jesus spake unto them, saying, Be of good cheer; it is I; be not afraid. (Matthew 14:22-27)

Prayer gave Jesus unrestricted access into the realm of the supernatural and it gave Him the capacity to suspend natural laws and see a demonstration of the mighty power of God.

The Transfiguration

The Transfiguration of Christ reveals spiritual truths about the power of prayer:

And it came to pass about an eight days after these sayings, he took Peter and John and James, and went up into a mountain to pray. And as he prayed, the fashion of his countenance was altered, and his raiment was white and glistering. (Luke 9:28-29)

You will realize that the transfiguration took place as He prayed. It was in the midst of prayer that the fashion of His countenance was altered. This was a divine metamorphosis or a supernatural change. When this occurred, Jesus and the disciples with Him began to enjoy supernatural manifestations.

- Elijah and Moses appeared unto them.
- They entered a cloud.
- They heard the voice of God.

When you take time to climb the mountains of spiritual ascendancy through fasting and prayer, you will experience supernatural change in different dimensions of your life. The things that seemed impossible will suddenly become possible.

Throughout His ministry, Jesus Christ had a lot of opposition from the Scribes and Pharisees. They always opposed Him with what the law and the prophets said. The main pillars behind the law and the prophets were Moses and Elijah and they were the ones that manifested themselves to Jesus Christ on the mount of transfiguration.

During times of intensive prayer, the main powers operating behind the scenes of any situation or opposition you are dealing with will manifest themselves but God will give you the victory. When those powers are revealed, you will begin to experience supernatural changes in different dimensions of your life. The things that seemed impossible will suddenly become divinely possible. Your purpose will be revealed and the promise will be fulfilled.

As He prayed, they entered the cloud. The presence of God overshadowed them and in the midst of the Presence of God the Voice of God was released. Through His lifestyle of prayer, Jesus has demonstrated the steps that are required to enter the Presence of God and what it is required to hear the Voice of God.

The Garden of Gethsemane

³⁹ And he came out, and went, as he was wont, to the mount of Olives; and his disciples also followed him.

⁴⁰ And when he was at the place, he said unto them, Pray that ye enter not into temptation.

⁴¹ And he was withdrawn from them about a stone's cast, and kneeled down, and prayed,

⁴² Saying, Father, if thou be willing, remove this cup from me: nevertheless not my will, but thine, be done.

⁴³ And there appeared an angel unto him from heaven, strengthening him.

⁴⁴ And being in an agony he prayed more earnestly: and his sweat was as it were great drops of blood falling down to the ground. (Luke 22: 39-44)

The battle for the redemption of humanity was won in the Garden of Gethsemane before Jesus Christ went to the cross at Calvary. His prayer was so intense and exacting that an angel had to come and strengthen him. Once he was reinvigorated, Jesus went into prayer so intense that, rather than sweat, His pores emptied great drops of blood falling onto the ground.

This is the length to which our Lord Jesus Christ believed in prayer. He won the victory in prayer before the battle began towards the cross.

If you will pray with fervency and intensity, you will win different dimensions of victory in the battles of life.

Jesus is Our Intercessor

Wherefore he is able also to save them to the uttermost that come unto God by him, seeing he ever liveth to make intercession for them.
(Hebrews 7:25)

One of the on-going ministries of our Lord Jesus Christ is the ministry of intercession. After He rose from the dead and ascended into heaven, He ascended as a high priest. One of His high priestly functions is that of an intercessor. As an intercessor He pleads with God on behalf of the saints of God and He prays for them.

It is important for you to know that Jesus is praying for you.

"By this, love is perfected with us, so that we may have confidence in the day of judgment; because as He is, so also are we in this world."
(1 John 4:17)

Intercession is the on-going current ministry of our Lord Jesus Christ. His ministry as an intercessor is part of His high priestly ministry that He performs for the present day believer and the Church. The prayers of Christ can make the difference in the vicissitudes of life. Only when we get to Heaven may we come to know all the traps and snares we have escaped because Christ prayed for us. The Bible says:

Simon, Simon, behold, Satan has demanded permission to sift you like wheat; but I have prayed for you, that your faith may not fail; and you, when once you have turned again, strengthen your brothers.
(Luke 22:31-32)

So don't give up! Don't stop praying. Don't be discouraged or grow weary. If you keep praying and remain faithful, you will get the victory. You are not alone in the battle and you will overcome by His Spirit, which has been made available to you. It's just a matter of time. The conditional requirement of our victory is that we don't give up. Let us wait for our due season as we tarry in prayer.

And let us not be weary in well doing: for in due season we shall reap, if we faint not. (Galatians 6:9)

Chapter Summary:

- Jesus Christ empowered us to use our Dominion Mandate by introducing and revealing to us the Kingdom of God

- Jesus Christ revealed the powers working behind the scenes and blocking our access to Heaven – he confronted and cast out demons

- Jesus Christ needed to fast and pray to master the flesh in His first battle with the devil

- Jesus Christ taught us that we must also master the flesh and keep constant fellowship through abiding in Him in order to live triumphantly

- Jesus prayed and was lead by the Holy Spirit. He was lead by the Spirit and filled with the Power of the Spirit

- Walking in the power of the Holy Ghost is a result of fasting, prayer and engaging the enemy.

- It is the Holy Spirit who teaches us to pray and what to pray for.

- Prayer gives us unrestricted access into the realm of the supernatural and causes us to experience supernatural change in different dimensions of life.

Chapter 11

Praying Strategic Prayers

"The [prayer] closet...is the battlefield of the Church; its citadel; the scene of heroic and unearthly conflicts." —, ***E.M. Bounds***

Prayer is a discipline and like every other good discipline, it must be developed. Prayer is a strategy that can be used to exercise our Dominion Mandate.

We are commanded to pray always and by daily practice we cultivate a consistent and fervent prayer life. By praying regularly, we acknowledge our need for God's help, His wisdom and guidance. It takes perseverance in prayer for His power to be released. The discipline of prayer, when it is practiced regularly can be infectious. Others around you will be infected and begin to increase their times of prayer as well.

The more you pray; you develop stamina and become sensitive to the Voice of God. Prayer is not just you speaking to God, but prayer involves God speaking back to you. Most people say they desire to know God's will for their life. I submit to you that His will (His expression of the future) is for you to pray. It is in the furnace of prayer that you will discover His purpose (what He intends for you to accomplish in the future) for your life.

We must not think that God will come to our rescue just because He sees that we need to be rescued. Many Christians do not believe in spiritual warfare. They do not believe that they must fight in order to obtain the prize. They are willing to live just having their salvation. But, salvation is not the inheritance. Being born again permits us to have salvation. This is our birthright. Every born again believer receives the free gift of salvation and becomes a part of the family. This is the power of the Blood of Jesus – to give us salvation and to make us a part of His family.

If you are born the son of Bill Gates or Warren Buffet, you have received the birthright through the bloodline. But receiving the benefits of inheritance goes beyond just being a blood relative. There are certain things you must know and certain things you must do in order to obtain your full inheritance. Bill Gates and Warren Buffet have done what it takes to build the wealth of their kingdoms. Their children must now do whatever their fathers command to receive the benefits of their fathers' labor. Often when the wealthy pass away and there is a will, there can be opposition. The will must be very clear. But, no matter how clear the will is, even the children must be able to raise a defense in the court of law against the opposition.

The Father, by sending the Son to die for us, has made a provision for us to receive all the wealth of the Kingdom. But Satan stands in opposition and resistance to keep us from taking back what belongs to us in the first place. This is why God said He hated Esau. Because Esau was willing to be cavalier about his inheritance as the firstborn and he lost it. Just like Adam, he let the appetite of his belly overpower his desire for his promised future. Scripture says:

> *And Jacob sod pottage: and Esau came from the field, and he was faint: And Esau said to Jacob, Feed me, I pray thee, with that same red pottage; for I am faint: therefore was his name called Edom. And Jacob said, Sell me this day thy birthright. And Esau said, Behold, I am at the point to die: and what profit shall this birthright do to me? And Jacob said, Swear to me this day; and he sware unto him: and he sold his birthright unto Jacob. Then Jacob gave Esau bread and pottage of lentils; and he did eat and drink, and rose up, and went his way: thus Esau despised his birthright. (Gen. 25:29-34)*

The principle to fast and pray is a divine key to help us be sensitive to the Voice of God so that we are not cavalier about the promises of God. We cannot act independent of God and believe we don't need Him. God hates the spirit of pride, which is what produces that independent spirit. Esau's prideful statement about the birthright and his cavalier independence caused him to immediately lose his identity and his name was changed from Esau to Edom in verse 30.

The judgment of God was swift and immediate, but the effects of the judgment took time. Our absolute dependence and obedience to the Voice of God is critical and we can avoid sudden calamity when we are sensitive to His desire for us. We can only develop this sensitivity in prayer. Without it, the offenses of life will harden our heart. When your heart is hardened you lack forgiveness. The lack of forgiveness produces bitterness. The bitterness provokes envy. Envy leads to anger. Anger leads to strife. Strife unchecked is capable of murder. You cannot pray with a hardened heart. God won't hear you when you don't forgive and you will grieve the Holy Spirit. Scripture says –

Do not grieve the Holy Spirit of God, by whom you were sealed for the day of redemption. Let all bitterness and wrath and anger and clamor and slander be put away from you, along with all malice. Be kind to one another, tender-hearted, forgiving each other, just as God in Christ also has forgiven you. (Ephesians 4:30-32)

As a leader with many sons and daughters, I love to forgive. I walk in the grace of forgiveness. I sow mercy because I need Mercy. I take every opportunity of betrayal and offense as an opportunity to exercise the virtue of forgiveness. This keeps my heart pliable and soft so that I can have access to the Holy Spirit and continue to be "sealed for the day of redemption." Mercy is what releases the Miracles of God's divine provision. In Psalm 23, King David says:

"You prepare a table before me in the presence of my enemies; You anoint my head with oil; My cup runs over. Surely goodness and mercy shall follow me all the days of my life; and I will dwell in the house of the Lord Forever."(Psalm 23:5-6)

The Hebrew translation of this portion of scripture is very powerful. It is translated:

The Lord honors His followers by setting a *shulcan* (a table) in the presence of *tsuris* – the word for those who trouble or aggravate you. The next word – *nes* -- means miracle.

Dashanti va-shemen roshi means you fatten my head with oil. *Adonai Jireh*: the Lord will provide.

So verse 5 means - The Lord will do a *miracle of provision* for me in the presence of those who *aggravate* me. The next verse translated in Hebrew is the phrase, *"Akh tov va-chesed yirdefuni kol-yemei chaiyai, ve-shavti be-veit-Adonai le-orekh yamim."* It means goodness and mercy will *chase* me back to *abide* in the House of the Lord forever.

Satan wants to use the weapons of betrayal and offense to cause you to operate in unforgiveness. He knows this is a direct hindrance to your prayers and shuts off your line of communication to the Father.

> *"And forgive us our debts, as we forgive our debtors. And lead us not into temptation, but deliver us from evil: For thine is the kingdom, and the power, and the glory, for ever. Amen. For if ye forgive men their trespasses, your heavenly Father will also forgive you: but if ye forgive not men their trespasses, neither will your Father forgive your trespasses." Matthew 6:12-15*

We don't get the kingdom, and the power, and the glory until we release the forgiveness. Friend, forgive anyone who has hurt you. Release it today so that your prayers will not be hindered. Prayers don't die. But they can be hindered.

> *"Thou hast covered thyself with a cloud, that our prayer should not pass through." (Lamentations 3:44)*

Unforgiveness is like a dry valley where unanswered prayers go until they are released by forgiveness. Unforgiveness wastes the most valuable thing you have in life: time. Forgive easily and without regret. But, most of all, forgive quickly.

Satan is the father of unforgiveness. When he was Lucifer, he had all the riches of Heaven at his disposal. He was a part of God's creation, but not a part of God's family. Jesus Christ is God's "only begotten Son."

Man was created as a part of God's family. That was the original plan. The Dominion Mandate is derived from that plan. We were made in the image of the Godhead and Jesus Christ has now reconciled us back to our original position. To be born again is to be reconciled to the Father.

"Therefore if any man be in Christ, he is a new creature: old things are passed away; behold, all things are become new. And all things are of God, who hath reconciled us to himself by Jesus Christ, and hath given to us the ministry of reconciliation; To wit, that God was in Christ, reconciling the world unto himself, not imputing their trespasses unto them; and hath committed unto us the word of reconciliation. Now then we are ambassadors for Christ, as though God did beseech you by us: we pray you in Christ's stead, be ye reconciled to God. For he hath made him to be sin for us, who knew no sin; that we might be made the righteousness of God in him." (2 Corinthians 5:17-21)

We are in the family of God! Our assignment according to verse 20 is to pray others into the family. Verse 20 says we are now the family ambassadors representing Christ coming to reconcile you to God the Father. To let you know, you have been adopted. You have been translated to another family. You have been transferred to another kingdom. Your adoption and your transfer are complete. The Amplified Bible says:

"For this reason we also, from the day we heard of it, have not ceased to pray and make [special] request for you, [asking] that you may be filled with the full (deep and clear) knowledge of His will in all spiritual wisdom [in comprehensive insight into the ways and purposes of God] and in understanding and discernment of spiritual things—

That you may walk (live and conduct yourselves) in a manner worthy of the Lord, fully pleasing to Him and desiring to please Him in all things, bearing fruit in every good work and steadily growing and increasing in and by the knowledge of God [with fuller, deeper, and clearer insight, acquaintance, and recognition].

[We pray] that you may be invigorated and strengthened with all power according to the might of His glory, [to exercise] every kind of endurance and patience (perseverance and forbearance) with joy,

Giving thanks to the Father, Who has qualified and made us fit to share the portion which is the inheritance of the saints (God's holy people) in the Light.

[The Father] has delivered and drawn us to Himself out of the control and the dominion of darkness and has transferred us into the kingdom of the Son of His love,

In Whom we have our redemption through His blood, [which means] the forgiveness of our sins." (Colossians 1:9-14)

You have been transferred. Your new assignment as a family ambassador is to pray for others to also receive their transfer. Now if that wasn't enough to convince you that you are in His family, Galatians 4:5-7 in the Message Bible says this:

"But when the time arrived that was set by God the Father, God sent his Son, born among us of a woman, born under the conditions of the law so that he might redeem those of us who have been kidnapped by the law. Thus we have been set free to experience our rightful heritage. You can tell for sure that you are now fully adopted as his own children because God sent the Spirit of his Son into our lives crying out, "Papa! Father!" Doesn't that privilege of intimate conversation with God make it plain that you are not a slave, but a child? And if you are a child, you're also an heir, with complete access to the inheritance."

We have to pray for others to be saved and receive the Spirit of adoption. We got in because someone prayed for us and our High Priest Jesus is now praying for us. We must continue to pray for others to be saved.

"My little children, of whom I travail in birth again until Christ be formed in you." (Galatians 4:19)

Here Paul says he must travail in birth *again* – this shows up that he prays for them to be saved and then he prays for them to be transformed.

That is why Satan works so hard to make sure that Christians don't pray. First, he tries to prevent us from learning we are a part of the family. When that doesn't work, he tries to block us from being able to get any survivors' benefits. He distracts us and keeps us busy with the cares of the world so that we forget we have an assignment in the Kingdom of God.

When we go to execute that assignment, he uses technicalities and legalities against us to steal, kill and destroy our prayer life. He will release an accusation against us and use guilt to move in position to enforce the judgment. But, we must use equally opposing force to defend our position to release the promises of our inheritance.

It is when we fight the good fight of faith through the discipline of prayer that we triumph over Satan and superimpose the Kingdom of God over the kingdom of darkness. This is the heritage of the servants of the Lord. This is how we enforce our Dominion Mandate. Scripture gives us a very important instruction. In Isaiah 54:17 it says:

> *"No weapon that is formed against thee shall prosper; and every tongue that shall rise against thee in judgment thou shalt condemn. This is the heritage of the servants of the Lord, and their righteousness is of me, saith the Lord."*

God is telling us that even though He has given us power over weapons fashioned against us, it doesn't mean the enemy won't try and use the weapon. He says that when the tongue of the accuser goes to execute the judgment of that weapon, it is our responsibility to condemn the judgment and that "our righteousness is of Him." That means our legal grounds to defend our position is backed by Him. God backs those who serve Him when they pray!

> *"To execute upon them the judgment written: this honour have all his saints. Praise ye the Lord." (Psalm 149:9)*

This is the way Jesus handled Satan after a 40-day fast in the wilderness. Satan still came and tried to use his weapons. They didn't work because Jesus condemned Satan with the

Word. This satanic encounter provides guidance for us to use in defeating the voice of Satan in times of spiritual warfare.

"And the devil said unto him, If thou be the Son of God, command this stone that it be made bread. And Jesus answered him, saying, It is written, That man shall not live by bread alone, but by every word of God. And the devil, taking him up into an high mountain, shewed unto him all the kingdoms of the world in a moment of time. And the devil said unto him, All this power will I give thee, and the glory of them: for that is delivered unto me; and to whomsoever I will I give it. If thou therefore wilt worship me, all shall be thine. And Jesus answered and said unto him, Get thee behind me, Satan: for it is written, Thou shalt worship the Lord thy God, and him only shalt thou serve. And he brought him to Jerusalem, and set him on a pinnacle of the temple, and said unto him, If thou be the Son of God, cast thyself down from hence: For it is written, He shall give his angels charge over thee, to keep thee: And in their hands they shall bear thee up, lest at any time thou dash thy foot against a stone. And Jesus answering said unto him, It is said, Thou shalt not tempt the Lord thy God. And when the devil had ended all the temptation, he departed from him for a season." (Luke 4:3-13)

Jesus' first spiritual battle was not to cast out demons. His first spiritual battle was to subdue His flesh through fasting and prayer. Jesus who came down from Glory and is the only man to have lived without sin, still had to take authority over the flesh through fasting and prayer.

Beloved, if our Saviour had to fast and pray to deal with Satan, how much more must those of us who are born-again believers do? We must discipline ourselves before we can deal with the tactics of the devil. We discipline the flesh through times of fasting and prayer.

Once Jesus mastered self-control and developed the stamina it takes to pray for 40 days in the wilderness without food or water, He was ready to take on the next battle and defeat Satan.

The defeat of Satan didn't come just because Jesus knew the Word. Satan was using the Word. The defeat came because He had developed the discipline to maintain His mission and stay focused on His purpose. He used the Word to reinforce the revelation of His purpose. What Satan was able to do to Eve in the Garden of Eden, he was not able to do to Jesus because of Jesus' continuous communication with the Father.

Jesus defeated Satan by removing all the comforts and accommodations of the flesh and maintaining a laser focus on accomplishing His assignment. This is what fasting and prayer does for us. Satan was not able to get Jesus to "second guess" God. Jesus knew God through a relationship of prayer and didn't permit Satan to define God's purpose for Him. This is what we must seek to develop as we build stamina in times of prayer.

Sometimes Christians don't see the need for unceasing prayer and may become complacent. Often they don't pray alone and regularly. They only pray when they are gathered with other believers, when they need something from God, or when there is a crisis. One of Satan's assignments is to hinder people from coming to Christ. If they come to Christ, he hinders them from being effective in their Christian walk. He gets them to be in a state of spiritual slumber and eventually a lack of awareness. But, we must be alert and enlightened to deal with the devices of Satan and destroy his plans. Examine the following scriptures:

Lest Satan should get an advantage of us: for we are not ignorant of his devices. (2 Corinthians 1:11)

My people are destroyed for lack of knowledge…. (Hosea 4:6a)

Besides this you know the time, that the hour has come for you to wake from sleep. For salvation is nearer to us now than when we first believed. The night is far gone; the day is at hand. So then let us cast off the works of darkness and put on the armor of light. (Romans 13:11-12)

Consider and hear me, O Lord my God: lighten mine eyes, lest I sleep the sleep of death. (Psalm 13:3)

Prayer is the most important privilege of a Christian and should be the heart desire of a new life in Christ. More is accomplished by prayer than has ever been accomplished by all the other "religious activities" in the world. It is by prayer that we enforce the "joy of His salvation." We repent in prayer and it is by prayer that we release the efficacy of the Blood of Jesus to wash us and purge us from all the uncleanness of iniquity and sin.

*"What a Friend we have in Jesus, all our sins and griefs to bear!
What a privilege to carry everything to God in prayer!
O what peace we often forfeit, O what needless pain we bear,
All because we do not carry everything to God in prayer."*
("What a Friend We Have in Jesus" – Joseph Scriven, 1855)

Prayer is dependence on God -- not on self. Jesus said, *"...man ought always to pray, and not faint"* (Luke 18:1). One does not need to receive a special call to have a ministry of prayer. To pray is as much a part of the Christian life as breathing is to the natural life. The disciples of Jesus did not ask Him to teach them to preach. They had one great request and that was, *"Lord, teach us to pray"* (Luke 11:1). You can be a prophet, a teacher, a pastor, an apostle, an evangelist, etc. but, without prayer life, you will eventually dry up, wither and disappear from the face of the Earth.

Saying prayers and praying are two different things. The self-righteous excel in saying prayers, but their utterings are without power. A person that allows the Holy Spirit to regenerate them enjoys this high calling of prayer; they take their position and access the Throne Room in power and authority through keys and principles that are deployed by praying.

Faith is essential in releasing the unlimited power of prayer. Jesus emphasized the necessity of faith in prayer as stated in Mark 11:23-24:

> *"For verily I say unto you, That whosoever shall say unto this mountain, Be thou removed, and be thou cast into the sea; and shall not doubt in his heart, but shall believe that those things which he saith shall come to pass; he shall have whatsoever he saith. Therefore I say unto you, What things soever ye desire, when ye pray, believe that ye receive them, and ye shall have them."*

In prayer, we discover the will of God, we build a strong relationship with God and we release the Word to confront obstacles and destroy barriers. The more we see victories in prayer, the stronger our faith becomes.

In prayer we fortify our faith, release angelic assistance to change the outcome of calamities and enforce the judgment written over the wicked. When we come to God in absolute faith, whatever we need, will be given to us in answer to our prayers. The Bible teaches that we must "ask, seek and knock" when we pray. Consistent, fervent prayers have tremendous power. A person who has great faith will also be a person who has a great prayer life.

The Apostle Paul says in 1 Thessalonians 5:17 *"Pray without ceasing."* He knew what it would take to co-labor with God and fulfill His calling and encouraged the young church full of new converts in Thessalonica by stressing the importance of prayer. He also understood that, unless the young church continued to mature in its faith, it was flirting with danger.

Romans 12:12 says *"Rejoicing in hope; patient in tribulation; continuing instant in prayer."* This was one of the keys Paul gave to the Roman Church which was under great persecution, that in times of difficulties and hardship they must be determined not to slack up in prayer but to stay in prevailing and constant communication with God.

In times of trouble, pray. In good times, pray. All the time, pray.

When Jesus battled Satan in the wilderness and won, the Bible says this:

> *"And when the devil had ended all the temptation, he departed from him for a season." (Luke 4:13)*

The devil was defeated in this battle so he left to go and regroup so he could try again. We must remember that our greatest victories are in front of us, not behind us. We must always remember that the kingdom of darkness is very well organized. Jesus gave us a divine key to deal with the organized kingdom of hell. He taught this parable:

> *"And he called them unto him, and said unto them in parables, How can Satan cast out Satan? And if a kingdom be divided against itself, that kingdom cannot stand. And if a house be divided against itself, that house cannot stand. And if Satan rise up against himself, and be divided, he cannot stand, but hath an end. No man can enter into a strong man's house, and spoil his goods, except he will first bind the strong man; and then he will spoil his house." (Mark 3:23-27)*

He told us that you must first deal with the strong man if you are going to get the victory. When we fail to uncover the wickedness and chaos hidden in the darkness, we are powerless to destroy the works of darkness. The only way to uncover and bind what is operating behind the scenes in a spiritual battle is to understand the powers that represent the strong man.

Knowledge is a key that will unlock the door to your greatest victory. I teach these principles on the hierarchy of Satan when I am training intercessors because it is necessary for you to know the strategies, capabilities and trusted weapons of your enemy. We have spent time teaching what prayer is capable of accomplishing, but knowing your enemy is what gives you the ability to pray strategic prayers.

The Infernal Kingdom

Both the Kingdom of God and that of Satan operate in hierarchical order. That is to say, there are grades of authority or status from the highest to the lowest ranks.

The Godhead also operates in order, and so do the angels of God who operate in various rankings with varying degrees of authority—chief or higher angels, lesser angels, in that order. We talked about the angels and know they are ready to provide assistance. But, we need to know the order of the powers of darkness so we know what weapons to deploy against that kingdom. We are dealing with two different kingdoms and their hierarchies.

The hierarchy mentioned in Colossians 1:16-17—*"For by Him all things were created that are in heaven and that are on earth, visible and invisible, whether thrones or dominions or principalities or powers. All things were created through Him and for Him*—is different from the satanic hierarchy mentioned in Ephesians 6:12: *"For we do not wrestle against flesh and blood, but against principalities and powers, against the rulers of darkness of this age, against spiritual hosts of wickedness in the heavenly places."*

Take note that "rulers of darkness of this age" and "spiritual hosts of wickedness in heavenly places" are not mentioned in the Colossians account.

God has angelic thrones with accompanying delegated authority in various capacities, according to their assigned duties. Satan, who has nothing originating from him other than evil, has sought to duplicate the divine order with a rival setup to carry out his evil schemes. We saw in the chapter on Esther how he used Haman. But, there was a power operating behind the scenes and influencing Haman from the spiritual realm.

Ephesians 6:12 tells us: *"For we do not wrestle against flesh and blood, but against principalities, against powers, against the rulers of darkness of this age, against spiritual hosts of wickedness in heavenly places."*

The above Scripture gives us insight about the structure and setup of Satan's kingdom. I will take you through these, and we will carefully examine each one of them according to their order of rankings and their varying degrees of authority and spheres of influence.

Principalities

This word is translated from a Greek word *archias*, meaning *a beginning* (the English word "archaic" originated from that Greek word), but was used to signify *a first rule*, or *a first principle*, and further, *a chief officer* of that principle, or the *territory* under its (or his) jurisdiction.

In Matthew 12:24, the devil is called "Beelzebub," meaning lord of the dwelling or domain in which these wicked spirits are subject to and operate under Satan's dwelling or domain. They, like their chief prince, direct, control, rule and carry out the present darkness of this world.

The *American Heritage Dictionary* defines principalities as:

1. A territory ruled by a prince or from which a prince derives his title.

2. The position, authority, or jurisdiction of a prince; sovereignty.

These are the princes of the underworld who manipulate certain sections of the universe. Principalities are ruling spirits assigned over nations and cities.

Principalities are the highest of the rankings in the enemy's domain. They have been given the power to influence the affairs of nations and kingdoms and to resist God's purposes concerning those nations and kingdoms.

They exert their influence over heads of nations and kings; and they seek to control the political lives of those nations, using the human head of the nation – its leader – as their main instrument of operation. They incite kings and rulers to pass wicked and unrighteous laws, most of which contravene the laws of Almighty God.

The infamous Adolf Hitler, who committed untold atrocities on the Jewish people, exterminating six million of them in

Nazi concentration camps, is an example of the work of principalities in modern history.

In Chapter 3, we read how the prayers of Rees Howells, other intercessors, corporate intercession and the strategies deployed by Sir Winston Churchill at the behest of an intercessor named Major Tudor-Pole were able to defeat Adolf Hitler's advances and override the powers working behind Hitler.

Scripture gives us a clear example of the strategy of principalities in Daniel, Chapter 10.

> *Then said he [the angel] unto me, Fear not, Daniel: for from the first day that thou didst set thine heart to understand, and to chasten [humble] thyself before thy God, thy words were heard, and I am come for thy words. But the prince of the kingdom of Persia withstood me one and twenty days: but, lo, Michael, one of the chief princes, came to help me; and I remained there with the kings of Persia.*
> *(Daniel 10:12-13)*

Gabriel, the messenger angel, came to deliver the answer to Daniel's prayer the first day Daniel began to pray. But, he was met with resistance and called for angelic reinforcements. The battle that took place and the resistance the enemy put up required Daniel to keep praying. His constant fasting and relentless prayers released the chief angel of God's angel army, Michael, to break the resistance. Archangel Michael is not mentioned often in scripture, but when he is referred to, he is in action. In the book of Daniel, Michael is battling wicked angels; in the letter of Jude, he is disputing Satan; and in Revelation, he is waging war with the devil and his demons.

Gabriel came with a message for Daniel from God, but in order to deliver the message he had to battle the resistance of the enemy. It is our prayers that create the necessary firepower to release angelic reinforcements. See what Gabriel said about their battle with, the prince of Persia:

> *Then said he [the angel], Knowest thou wherefore I come unto thee? and now will I return to fight with the prince of Persia: and when I am gone forth, lo, the prince of Grecia shall come. But I will shew thee that which is noted in the scripture of truth: and there is none that holdeth with me in these things, but Michael your prince. (Dan 10:20-21)*

Beloved, this battle and the associated prophecy is still studied today by historians and Bible scholars alike. History tells us that approximately 250 years after this prophecy, the Persian Kingdom with all its might and power, fell to a great warrior from Greece by the name of Alexander the Great. There was a spiritual principality that was ruling an earthly king to bring about the wickedness that Daniel confronted with imprecatory prayers and the word of prophecy.

Our battle is not carnal, but it is spiritual. Even when you can't see what your prayers are doing, they are working. When an intercessor dies, their prayers continue to reverberate through time and eternity. Daniel was gone, but his 21 days of intercessory prayers and the prophecy continued reverberating for 250 years and beyond.

The battle with the prince of Persia was completed during the 21 days of Daniel's fasting and prayers. Gabriel reported back to his position to watch over the kings of Persia. Eventually, another wicked principality came -- the prince of Grecia. A new wicked principality came and a new earthly king reigned. Alexander the Great came on the scene.

You must pray for the leaders of your nation. While there is a wicked principality over a region or nation, this passage tells us that there is a watchman angel waiting to be deployed by your prayers! Your prayers can have great impact on the future and destiny of your nation. You release angelic assistance over your nation's leadership when you give voice to the Word of God. Paul told us to pray for kings so we can live in peace.

> *Therefore I exhort first of all that supplications, prayers, intercessions, and giving of thanks be made for all men, for kings and all who are in authority, that we may lead a quiet and peaceable life in all godliness and reverence. For this is good and acceptable in the sight of God our Savior. (1 Timothy 2:1-3)*

If you don't pray for your leader to receive angelic assistance and you just complain about what the leader is doing, you bind the help of the angel who watches over the nation to bring prosperity and peace. Additionally, your words can empower the wicked principality to exact punishment over the entire nation.

Gabriel told Daniel that even though he heard him on the first day of his prayers and went to help him, he was resisted. He was battling on his own until the Archangel Michael came and the resistance broke because of the words of Daniel! He says, "I came for your words."

It is your persistent, constant and continual words spoken in prayer that break the resistance of Satan and his princes. This is a great revelation on the power of intercession and the effect of an intercessor who will build stamina and enter into perpetual prayer. It took 21 days to set in motion a victory that remained intact for 250 years and beyond. Your prayers are important, so no matter what you see or don't see, keep on praying!

The devil controls the kingdoms of the world and we are not to underestimate his influence and power, nor believe that this is the will of God. God is telling us to "stand" against these evil forces by equipping ourselves with the power of God, and looking unto Christ as our example.

And the devil, taking him (Jesus) up into an high mountain, shewed unto him all the kingdoms of the world in a moment of time. And the devil said unto him, All this power will I give thee, and the glory of them: for that is delivered (to surrender or yield up) unto me; and to whomsoever I will I give it. If thou therefore wilt worship me, all shall be thine. (Luke 4:5-7)

These "kingdoms" the devil was speaking of represent his realm of rulership. He was showing Christ his territory – stolen territory acquired through deception and high treason in the Garden of Eden. At the end of this age, it is this territory – the kingdoms of this world – that the Church will have regained and subdued by prayer and by wrestling in intercession. John said in Revelation:

> *And the seventh angel sounded; and there were great voices in heaven, saying, The kingdoms of this world are become the kingdoms of our Lord, and of his Christ; and he shall reign for ever and ever.*
> *(Revelation 11:15)*

Apostle Paul tells us that we do not wrestle with flesh and blood, but with principalities or peoples or regions under the influence and deception of Satan. Satan is the prince or ruler of the kingdoms of this world, also described in the Bible as the "kingdom of darkness," in which we have our spiritual warfare.

The Powers

Powers is the second level of authority in Satan's kingdom. They exert their influence over the decision-making bodies of a nation, influencing the structures of all the governing authorities and promoting wickedness and injustice by controlling lawmakers, policy makers, and counselors in places of authority in the land. These powers represent the mighty princes of all the infernal legions. Great is their power, and that of the legions they command.

In the Book of Daniel, it was the counselors and governors who went to the king to report on Daniel's prayer life. These second-tier leaders, by working behind the scenes, were able to interfere with Daniel's favor and to incite the king against Daniel without cause.

Daniel had been a slave in the Persian kingdom. But, when God looked for someone to speak to, he bypassed the king and located Daniel. It reminds us that we must not despise our position in this world. If we commit ourselves to prayer, God will make sure our position represents His strategic plan to bring about His purposes.

Like Joseph, Daniel was a prisoner one day and a high-ranking government official the next. In a sort of overnight cabinet shakeup, Daniel became the prime minister. He became the master of those same men who had conspired against him.

When the powers found Daniel whose divine assignment would free the Jews from captivity, destroy the works of darkness and prophesy the end of the age, they went into overdrive to thwart the mission. In some cases, they don't just target one person, but a whole nation or even an entire generation.

We see this happen in families, in churches, in communities and even in nations. The powers behind the scenes work to stir up leadership against the righteous with wicked provocations spoken in secret.

Beloved, sometimes your warfare is commensurate with your assignment. But, when you know your enemy and his strategy – you can battle more effectively.

Powers influence the thoughts and feelings of human beings. They can influence people to kill, steal, and indulge in all manner of destructive deeds. Friends, these powers can even influence Christians to gossip, to backbite, to slander people, to bear grudges against each other, even cause people to eat too much or cause them not to fast, or influence persons to abstain from church activities.

They cause people to have a lackadaisical attitude toward the work of God and convince them to spend more time watching television than reading their Bibles. These powers can draw Christians away from paying tithes—or should they intend to pay tithes, they are influenced not to pay the correct amount. The list can go on. These examples are cited to illustrate some of the influencing operations of the powers—even among believers.

The word "power" also denotes delegated authority. This category of Satan's hierarchy uses delegated demonic authority to destroy peace and love between ministers, between pastors and congregation members, between Christians within the same church, between various churches or between denominations. They promote strife and contention amidst the Christian community.

They also exert influence in families to cause strife and division. They are responsible for divorces and the breakdown of family unions. In the natural, we can point to the carnal causes, but in the spirit, there were powers working behind the scenes.

They influence gangs and devilish fraternities and are responsible for the unruly behavior of certain individuals in educational institutions and within the society.

Powers make Christians believe a lie and get into a state of offense. They work through the media and promote Satan's agenda via the airwaves and the newspapers. Remember, one of Satan's titles is "the prince of the power of the air" (Ephesians 2:2).

It is these powers that are released against the person who is anointed, but who hasn't developed the character that matches their anointing. They will influence the person to misbehave and then expose the behavior to cause the person to lose their position of favor. They use long-range strategies. They are looking for an occasion to bring a provocation.

Rulers of Darkness

Next in the satanic hierarchy are the rulers of darkness of this age (Ephesians 6:12). The word used in original Greek is *kosmokrateros*, which means *world rulers*. The word *kosmos* denotes *order* or *arrangement*, whereas the word *kratos* has to do with *raw power*. Thus, the compounded word, *kosmokrateros*, depicts *raw power that has been harnessed and put into some kind of order*.

This same word *kosmokrateros* was at times used to picture military training camps where young men were assembled, trained, and turned into a mighty army. These young men were like raw power when they first arrived in the training camp. However, as the military training progressed and the new recruits were taught discipline and order, all that raw manpower was converted into an organized, disciplined army.

This is the word Paul now uses in his description of Satan's kingdom. This group – the Rulers of Darkness – comes after the Powers in hierarchy but before the lower level ground troops. These are managers of generational curses and they hold the records of accusation over the lives of individuals, families, churches, territories and nations. They give out assignments to the lower levels and deploy reinforcements generation after generation. These are the Navy Seals and snipers of Satan's hierarchy.

The rulers of darkness are mandated by the devil to promote false religions and occult practices, thereby enslaving the souls of men in deception. It is not at all strange to see kings and rulers of nations striving to enforce false religions upon their people. In some nations, the penalty for being a Christian is death. Islam is one such ruler of darkness. These satanic record keepers are responsible to make sure that if Christianity takes territory in one generation in a specific location, they will plan and strategize to take that territory back in the next generation. They are trained in the art of causing blindness and slumber to rest over entire nations.

This is the force behind terrorist groups. This is the blinding veil that deceives men to believe a lie that drives them to commandeer a passenger plane and fly hundreds of people to a fiery death. This is the force that drives people to walk in a school in Kenya and target Christians in a mass murder. This is the ruler that pushes a minority of the people to seize a larger group of people in an entire village in Nigeria and have them line up to be systematically murdered if they do not renounce the Name of Jesus and throw away their faith. It is the same ruler of darkness that clouds the minds of men to believe in the supremacy of one race over another to the point where no lives truly matter.

Friend, the main aim of these rulers of darkness is to control. They deceive human beings and place in their minds false teachings, false visions, and false dreams. They promote astrology, numerology, palmistry, fortune telling, divinations, horoscope, hypnotism, witchcraft, black and white magic, conjuration, charms, fetishes, and incantation. They also promote false religions such as Buddhism, Taoism, Hinduism, Islam, Shintoism, Confucianism, Eckankar, and the Baha'i faith.

Spiritual Host of Wickedness

This word *"wickedness"* is different than the person who is wicked – That word is *rasha,* defined earlier in reference to *"the wicked"* and denoting the wicked character of a person who is against God.

But this word *"wickedness"* is taken from the word *ponēros*, and it is used to depict *something that is bad, vile, malevolent, vicious, impious, and malignant.* These are evil spirits, personalities who host the embodiment of evil. They cause calamity and sudden destruction.

These spiritual hosts of wickedness in heavenly realms have oversight to enforce wicked decrees and judgments. They look through the records of a family to decide what to inflict upon the next generation. Their assignment against a person starts from the womb. They represent the satanic horns that fight families, churches, and territories with long battles and unnecessary distractions that drain wealth and time and keep men from coming to salvation, being fruitful in their walk with Christ. And they hinder people from praying.

They promote lawlessness and wickedness in the land, ensnaring souls of men into all manner of abominable sins, such as homosexuality, lesbianism, rape, all manner of lust and lasciviousness, suicides, and drug addiction, to mention but a few. They cast spells and are responsible to monitor lives to ensure we believe the lie of the devil concerning whatever vice they have deployed against us.

Seeking a promotion, they go through great extremes to please the higher levels. They delight in bringing down the righteous with secret sins and they use information to torment and inflict great pain related to iniquity. These are the spirits that hold you down in your sleep, torment you in your mind, have sex with you in dreams, make you do things that you otherwise would never do – and then after all that – convince you that you are guilty and that God will not receive you if you call on Him. They are the wicked *seat of power* behind the wickedness of the wicked.

This category is sometimes difficult to identify. The key to their operations resides in the word *wickedness*. Witches and witchcraft operations are under this group. Also in this category are marine and water spirits—Satan's navy. The witches and territorial spirits are Satan's air force, and demons form his troops.

Spiritual wickedness is responsible for accidents, premature death, suicides, and the like. They delay the blessings of God's people through situations and circumstances that are orchestrated against them. They are responsible for unseen obstacles that retard the progress and advancement of God's people. They enforce satanic setbacks and delight in vain labor.

The Eyes of Your Understanding

Beloved, may the eyes of your understanding be enlightened by this information. I pray that you have found a new reason to pray and developed new weapons of warfare. Let this Word be your guide and encourage you that as long as you fight, you will win.

"That the God of our Lord Jesus Christ, the Father of glory, may give unto you the spirit of wisdom and revelation in the knowledge of him: The eyes of your understanding being enlightened; that ye may know what is the hope of his calling, and what the riches of the glory of his

inheritance in the saints, and what is the exceeding greatness of his power to us-ward who believe, according to the working of his mighty power, which he wrought in Christ, when he raised him from the dead, and set him at his own right hand in the heavenly places, far above all principality, and power, and might, and dominion, and every name that is named, not only in this world, but also in that which is to come: and hath put all things under his feet, and gave him to be the head over all things to the church, which is his body, the fulness of him that filleth all in all." (Ephesians 1:18-23)

Chapter Summary

- Prayer is a discipline that must be developed and you can deploy strategy in prayer when you know the weapons of your warfare and the opponents of your battle

- You are a member of God's Family and you have an inheritance.

- You must contend for the will because Satan stands against you in opposition

- You cannot be cavalier about this contention. It was so serious that God sent Christ to die for you to inherit the Kingdom and be reconciled to Him.

- Your disobedience and your neglect of using the principles of the Kingdom can grieve the Holy Spirit.

- Satan uses the weapons of betrayal, offense and unforgiveness to block our prayers

- You must first deal with the strong man and uncover the wickedness and chaos hidden in the darkness and operating behind the scenes

The Infernal Kingdom

Ephesians 6:12 tells us: *"For we do not wrestle against flesh and blood, but against principalities, against powers, against the rulers of darkness of this age, against spiritual hosts of wickedness in heavenly places."*

In summary, the functions of Principalities are:

- Detailing and directing plans for countries and cities.
- Influencing men and women in government and positions of national decision-making.
- Directly carrying out the evil purposes of Satan.

In summary, the Powers have the ability to:

- Influence the thoughts and feelings of human beings.
- Influence Christians for destructive purposes.
- Influence and operate through the media and public information outlets.

In summary, the Rulers of Darkness are there to:

- Control human beings through deception and mind control

- Deceive human beings through false teachings, false visions, and false dreams

- Promote astrology, numerology, palmistry, fortune telling, divinations, horoscope, hypnotism, witchcraft, black and white magic, conjuration, charms, fetishes, and incantation.

- Promote false religions

- Keep satanic records

- Take back lost territory generation to generation

In summary, the Spiritual Hosts of Wickedness are assigned to:

- They are very injurious and destructive in nature.

- They may appear as angels of light; and by their deception they draw many souls into their nets of destruction.

- They sometimes try to influence and interfere with messages from the pulpit. They cause Christians to sleep during the preaching of the Word of God and are responsible for distracting their concentration at church services, depriving them of spiritual insight.

- They convince the unsaved that all is well with them.

Chapter 12

Covenant Prayer Keys

"The yearning to know what cannot be known, to comprehend the incomprehensible, to touch and taste the unapproachable, arises from the image of God in the nature of man. Deep calleth unto deep, and though polluted and landlocked by the mighty disaster theologians call the Fall, the soul senses its origin and longs to return to its source." –
A.W. Tozer

There are many different types of prayers revealed in the Bible. Christ is interceding for us now. The Holy Spirit intercedes on our behalf.

Jesus always prayed while He was on Earth and He promised the Holy Spirit would come to give us power with the evidence being revealed in prayer. Beloved, it is prayer alone that moves God! Preaching, teaching, and prophecy is for the Church in the Earth. It will move men. But, without prayer, none of those things will move God. Without moving God, those gifts are exercised in vain.

He wants us to bear fruit and fruit that will remain. But, He gave us the key for this to happen:

Abide in me, and I in you. As the branch cannot bear fruit of itself, except it abide in the vine; no more can ye, except ye abide in me.

I am the vine, ye are the branches: He that abideth in me, and I in him, the same bringeth forth much fruit: for without me ye can do nothing.

If a man abide not in me, he is cast forth as a branch, and is withered; and men gather them, and cast them into the fire, and they are burned.

If ye abide in me, and my words abide in you, ye shall ask what ye will, and it shall be done unto you.

Herein is my Father glorified, that ye bear much fruit; so shall ye be my disciples. (John 15:4-8)

This is the key to answered prayer. This is the key to exercising the Dominion Mandate and gaining access to our Covenant blessings. We can be in Christ and still live a life that is unfruitful – a life filled with unanswered prayers.

Living a life that is <u>fruitful</u> is *conditional*. There are many Christians today who struggle to pray and who cannot tell you assuredly that their prayers are answered.

But, Jesus tells us here in John 15 that if we are to be fruitful, we must *abide* in Him. What does it mean to abide in Him?

Abide in Him – The Key to Answered Prayer

The abiding Christian receives a major benefit from Jesus, namely, answered prayer. Abiding is a daily choice. Jesus says in John 15:7:

> *"If you abide in Me, and My words abide in you, then you shall ask whatever you desire, and it shall be done for you."*

The "if" reveals to us that abiding is *conditional*. You may or you may not abide. It is a daily choice we must make.

The Greek term used here is *menō* and is generally translated to mean "to abide," "to remain," "to stand fast," "to wait," "to hold your position."

In the upper room, Jesus uses the term 14 times in His final message to the disciples. Apostle John uses the term 34 times in the Gospel and 19 times in his letters. He is known as the Apostle whom Jesus loved. John 13:23, 25 says:

> *Now there was leaning on Jesus' bosom one of his disciples, whom Jesus loved.... He then lying on Jesus' breast saith unto him, Lord, who is it?*

The disciple was asking Christ a personal question about who among them would be the betrayer. His position indicates his proximity and his desire to have communion or continual fellowship with the Lord. But, it is the answer he received that intimates and validates that his desire to *abide* produced a hidden key to answered prayer:

> **Jesus answered, He it is, to whom I shall give a sop, when I have dipped it. And when he had dipped the sop, he gave it to Judas Iscariot, the son of Simon. And after the sop Satan entered into him. Then said Jesus unto him, 'That thou doest, do quickly.' Now no man at the table knew for what intent he spake this unto him. (John 13:26-28)**

Beloved, when you are willing to abide in Jesus, He will reveal prophetic secrets to you. He will trust you with things others do not know and cannot hear even though they are in His presence. This passage shows us that to be *in Christ* is not the same as *abiding in Christ*.

All twelve of the disciples were in the room with Christ. But, it is John alone who received the insight and answer from Christ about this particular secret. He is the only one besides

Christ who knew who the betrayer was. To be in Christ, you will receive salvation. But, it is *abiding in Christ* that releases the benefits of our Kingdom inheritance. Not every believer gets access to the benefits of their inheritance. If you choose not to pray every day, you choose not to abide in Him.

In the preceding verses, we see Christ give His disciples a prophetic illustration of the necessity of being in Him daily.

In the illustration in John 13, the Saviour of the world disrobes and ties a cloth around His waist and bends down in humility to wash his disciples' feet. Peter, like many of us when we receive salvation, is smug and says, "You don't need to do all that," in much the way that other believers might tell us "you don't need to do all that" when we enter into prayer and fasting.

You may receive challenges from other Christians when you take a radical stand to draw nearer to the Lord. They will try and convince you that the way you are going about it, is not the right way or is unnecessary.

> *Peter saith unto him, Thou shalt never wash my feet. Jesus answered him, If I wash thee not, thou hast no part with me. Simon Peter saith unto him, Lord, not my feet only, but also my hands and my head. Jesus saith to him, He that is washed needeth not save to wash his feet, but is clean every whit: and ye are clean, but not all. (John 13:8-10)*

At this point, Christ had not gone to the Cross yet. The magnitude of the work of the Cross – in forgiving and pardoning sin – is not yet a revelation to the disciples. They will come to understand that salvation is a result of the forgiveness of sin; that forgiveness is the cleansing and washing away of the original sin and it was completed on the Cross:

> *For we know that since Christ was raised from the dead, he cannot die again; death no longer has mastery over him. The death he died, he died to sin once for all; but the life he lives, he lives to God.*
> *(Romans 6:9-10)*

Jesus died once for all, to bring us to the point of justification. But, it is what we do to maintain that relationship that reflects and releases the efficacy of our continual fellowship with Him.

Although all sin is forgiven at the Cross, the washing of their feet is indicative of their need for daily fellowship to remain in communion with the Saviour. To abide in Him requires daily fellowship. We do this in prayer. We release His abiding presence when we pray daily and commune with Him in the realm of the Spirit.

If you live a life of prayerlessness, you run the risk of not having a relationship with God. Without this intimacy, you can be easily challenged by Satan and the hierarchy of his kingdom described in the previous chapter. This lack of fellowship with the Source of our salvation will prevent us from being fruitful.

We can only bear fruit and be fruitful – exercise the Dominion Mandate – in prayer. Prayer is a daily necessity for daily triumph. Jesus said:

I am the vine, ye are the branches: He that <u>abideth</u> in me, and I in him, the same bringeth forth much fruit: for without me ye can do nothing. (John 15:5)

The Lord is saying He is our Source. If we are connected to the Source, we will bear much fruit. But, without Him we can do nothing.

If ye abide in me, and my words abide in you, ye shall ask what ye will, and it shall be done unto you. (John 15:7)

We have said the term *menō* translates to "to abide," "to remain," "to stand fast," "to wait," "to hold your position." That means that we must be willing to remain in a posture of waiting until the Lord instructs us. What this Scripture tells us is that if we do that, we will always receive an answer to what we have prayed. Indeed, it is no longer us praying. It is the Lord praying through us. This is the power of an intercessor. An intercessor lays down his own will to pick up the will of Christ and this is what the Father responds to. He responds by sending the Holy Spirit to pray through you to manifest His will in the earth. The Bible says:

Likewise the Spirit also helpeth our infirmities: for we know not what we should pray for as we ought: but the Spirit itself maketh intercession for us with groanings which cannot be uttered. And he that searcheth the hearts knoweth what is the mind of the Spirit, because he maketh intercession for the saints according to the will of God. (Romans 8:26-27)

The assignment of the Holy Spirit in prayer is to tell us what to pray, as well as, to pray for us according to the will of God. It is the mind of the Spirit that provides revelation of things to come and causes us to have a fruitful prayer life. We must spend time waiting for Him and being led by Him. That is the life of a believer. We are saved, being saved and we shall be saved.

The first thing to be saved is the spirit. You were saved at the moment of conversion.

> *In him you also, when you heard the word of truth, the gospel of your salvation, and believed in him, were sealed with the promised Holy Spirit. (Ephesians 1:13)*

So your spirit is saved. But, your mind must be transformed. The Bible says:

> *And be not conformed to this world: but be ye transformed by the renewing of your mind, that ye may prove what is that good, and acceptable, and perfect, will of God. (Romans 12:2)*

Your mind requires daily renewal. Your body will ultimately be glorified when you see Christ:

> *Beloved, now are we the sons of God, and it doth not yet appear what we shall be: but we know that, when he shall appear, we shall be like him; for we shall see him as he is. And every man that hath this hope in him purifieth himself, even as he is pure. (1 John 3:2-3)*

Scripture clearly indicates that as believers we have a responsibility to purify ourselves.

In order to abide in Christ; we must be willing to "watch and pray" until our answer is made clear. It is this ability to watch and pray as we abide in Him that produces the answer to prayer. His ultimate and final betrayal shows us the importance of watching and praying.

> *They went to a place called Gethsemane, and Jesus said to his disciples, "Sit here while I pray." He took Peter, James and John along with him, and he began to be deeply distressed and troubled. "My soul is overwhelmed with sorrow to the point of death," he said to them. "Stay here and keep watch." (Mark 14:32-34)*

This shows us that in times of prayer, there are levels we can enter with the Lord. The Lord needed to enter into travailing prayers. He didn't take all the disciples. He took the ones He had spent the most time with. He told the others to wait for Him to return. But, He instructed Peter, James and John to "stay here and keep watch." He wanted them to abide in Him. To watch with Him. To enter the realm of intercession and take on His burden.

In Mark 14:35-36, He asks the Father to let the "cup pass from Him." He is distressed and wants to be backed in prayer. He returns to find them sleeping and rebukes them:

> *Then he returned to his disciples and found them sleeping. "Simon," he said to Peter, "are you asleep? Couldn't you keep watch for one hour? Watch and pray so that you will not fall into temptation. The spirit is willing, but the flesh is weak. (Mark 14:37-38)*

He tells Peter that if you don't watch and pray, you will fall into temptation. The spirit is willing but the flesh is weak. We bring the flesh under subjection in prayer.

We must remain vigilant or we will give the devil a foothold (Ephesians 4:27). The last time Jesus returns to his slumbering disciples, He lets them know they have failed the test – this time.

When he came back, he again found them sleeping, because their eyes were heavy. They did not know what to say to him. (Mark 14:40)

In Jesus' first spiritual lesson, He shows us how to subdue the flesh and operate in the realm of the Spirit by prayer and fasting. In this final warning, He shows us that if we don't watch and pray and we permit the flesh to master the spirit, we will give place to the devil and be caught unaware. We will permit the blinding veil of Satan to cause us to lack illumination and sleep the sleep of death:

Consider and hear me, O Lord my God: lighten mine eyes, lest I sleep the sleep of death. (Psalm 13:3)

Beloved, if the following covenant prayer keys are going to work for you – you must be willing to abide in Christ, pray with revelation from the Spirit, allowing God to pray through you as *you watch and pray.*

The Prayer of Faith

The prayer of faith is called the prayer of petition. This prayer is what people all over the world in every religion pray. Faith is a principle and everyone has faith in something. The Bible says in Romans 12:3, "For I say, through the grace given unto me, to every man that is among you, not to think of himself more highly than he ought to think; but to think soberly, according as God hath dealt to every man the measure of faith."

It is by faith that we pray and obtain the things for which we pray. This is a principle that works for everyone in all religions and whether what they pray for is good or bad. Faith is a principle. Your faith represents your belief in a particular outcome. This is why even atheists pray. They may not call it prayer and they certainly don't pray to God. They may call it by another name and say it is "thoughts," meditation, luck or some other name. But, it is the principle of their measure of faith in action that produces whatever they desire.

The key verses for the prayer of faith is Mark 11:22-24, in which Jesus says, "And Jesus answering saith unto them, Have faith in God. For verily I say unto you, That whosoever shall say unto this mountain, Be thou removed, and be thou cast into the sea; and shall not doubt in his heart, but shall believe that those things which he saith shall come to pass; he shall have whatsoever he saith. Therefore I say unto you, What things soever ye desire, when ye pray, believe that ye receive them, and ye shall have them."

The prayer of faith is answered by the level of belief that we have in the One to whom we are asking to answer our prayer. Have faith in God.

Hebrews 11:1 says, "Now faith is the substance of things hoped for, the evidence of things not seen." Your faith is substance; it is something real, something tangible. It is evidence of things you cannot see.

Notice that Mark 11:24 does not say when you will actually see the result of your prayer. It does not tell you how long it will take for that prayer result to appear, and this is where many Christians get hung up.

God lives in eternity and He is not governed by time or distance. When we pray, if we have faith in Him, we know that we have what we have prayed for, and we will see "the travail of our soul." This means that it is now just a matter of time before manifestation of our prayer request.

When you pray in faith, God immediately releases an answer to your prayer in the spirit realm. But in the natural world, due to a number of factors, it may take time for the answer to manifest itself.

God answers prayers, and He will answer your specific prayer in line with His Word, but it is the prayer of faith that brings that answer out of the spiritual world and into the physical world.

So shall my word be that goeth forth out of my mouth: it shall not return unto me void, but it shall accomplish that which I please, and it shall prosper in the thing whereto I sent it. (Isaiah 55:11)

Here we see the operation of God's Word. He says when He sends His Word forth, He sends it on assignment. When we pray and use His Word, we send that same Word back to Him to stand in His court and give an account for the purpose for which He spoke it. It must prosper and accomplish what He sent it to do. It is when that Word passes from the realm of the Spirit, *through our faith*, back into the earth realm, that we see the manifestation of its purpose.

Now faith is the substance of things hoped for, the evidence of things not seen. (Hebrews 11:1)

In order for the invisible substance of the Word to materialize, it must pass through the furnace of our faith. Our faith is what gives the Word the power to operate in the earth realm. The level of our belief in God is what determines the power of our faith to manifest the things for which we are praying.

Now unto him that is able to do exceeding abundantly above all that we ask or think, according to the power that worketh in us. (Ephesians 3:20)

The prayer of faith denotes that you are directing your request to someone you believe can make it happen. That's why Jesus said – Have faith in God. This permits not just what you want, but what God desires to come to pass. Which is why God will do more than we can ask or think, because now we have prayed in faith and He is making it happen by His power at work in us.

Sometimes when I am praying, I will hear the Holy Spirit say "pray this" or "pray that" and He will change the direction of my prayer. When I hear Him and I do what I hear, I know the prayer will be answered. It is not because I believe in my prayers. It is because, it is not *me* praying, it is Him praying through me. I know I will see the travail of my soul because I believe in the Father and I know if He says it, He will do it.

The prayer of faith will work for you if you have faith in God.

Corporate Prayer

Many people confuse corporate prayer with the Prayer of Agreement. But they are very different. Often, we may be praying corporately with others, but that doesn't mean we are praying a prayer of agreement. Jesus told this story of two men praying in the temple:

> *Two men went up into the temple to pray; the one a Pharisee, and the other a publican. The Pharisee stood and prayed thus with himself, God, I thank thee, that I am not as other men are, extortioners, unjust, adulterers, or even as this publican. I fast twice in the week, I give tithes of all that I possess. And the publican, standing afar off, would not lift up so much as his eyes unto heaven, but smote upon his breast, saying, God be merciful to me a sinner. (Luke 18:10-13)*

Both men are in church (the temple) and both men are praying to God. And possibly the prayer topic was repentance. But, their individual approaches in this corporate setting were very different.

This is what happens on Sunday mornings in most churches. We join in prayer and maybe even pray about the same topic, but our approaches are still individual and based on our position in our various situations.

Corporate prayer involves praying with others for the same purpose. But, unless everyone prays aloud individually before the whole group, you can't know whether there is truly agreement. We may all be praying about marriage. Some of us are praying to get in; some of us are praying to get out. We are praying together on the same topic, but we are not necessarily in agreement.

Peter was arrested and in Acts 12:5 it says, "Peter therefore was kept in prison: but prayer was made without ceasing of the church unto God for him." The church lifted up corporate prayers to enforce the release of Peter. An angel was dispatched from Heaven and Peter was miraculously released that night. When he got to the gate of the house where they were meeting, the Bible says:

> *And as Peter knocked at the door of the gate, a damsel came to hearken, named Rhoda. And when she knew Peter's voice, she opened not the gate for gladness, but ran in, and told how Peter stood before the gate. And they said unto her, Thou art mad. But she constantly affirmed that it was even so. Then said they, It is his angel. But Peter continued knocking: and when they had opened the door, and saw him, they were astonished. (Acts 12:13-16)*

They were gathered and praying so earnestly – at least, some of them -- that an angel was released. But upon the appearance of their prayer request and seeing the answer to their prayer in the flesh, the Bible says the young girl Rhoda was confused, those who heard the report were unbelieving and the collective group was astonished that the prayer had been answered. This is what can happen when we are praying corporately.

The Bible describes corporate prayer in Acts 2:42, which says "They devoted themselves to the apostles' teaching and to the fellowship, to the breaking of bread and to prayer."

When Jesus ascended, everyone who had witnessed His ascension joined in corporate prayer. "These all continued with one accord in prayer and supplication, with the women, and Mary the mother of Jesus, and with his brethren" (Acts 1:14). It is these corporate prayers that established the foundation of the Early Church and have propagated through all these generations to the church today.

When church members gather for learning, encouragement and fellowship, they may pray together to enforce their common mission and common goals. That is what we experience on Sunday morning in a worship service. It is very powerful when we have all things in common, when we have small group gatherings and pray with other like-minded believers in a larger setting. People are edified and united in a common bond of faith. They may also worship and have a time of repentance as a corporate body of believers.

Corporate prayer is important and people who have not developed a prayer discipline are most familiar with it. One of its benefits is that it helps you develop a discipline and it certainly helps grow your faith as you fellowship with other believers.

But, as you can see from scripture, it is not the most effective method of prayer unless you are sure you are all of one mind and one heart praying the same thing in the same place.

Beloved, I submit to you that often in corporate prayer we can be desensitized to the prayers of others. We forget that this is the time to pray for the greater good of all the people. When you gather with your church this Sunday or whatever day you go, determine that when the Pastor or leader asks for everyone to pray a particular prayer topic that you will join in faith to pray. Remember to pray not just so that you alone can be blessed, but, pray that you can be a blessing.

The Prayer of Agreement

The Prayer of Agreement is not the same as corporate prayer. It is exponentially more powerful.

Jesus introduced the prayer of agreement when He said:

> *Again I say unto you, That if two of you shall agree on earth as touching any thing that they shall ask, it shall be done for them of my Father which is in heaven. For where two or three are gathered together in my name, there am I in the midst of them. (Matthew 18:19)*

In order for the prayer of agreement to work, the people involved in the prayer have to be in agreement for what they are praying. Additionally, very often people misquote this passage of scripture. The translation doesn't say the two people have to touch each other. It says you must believe "**_as touching_** any thing that they shall ask". This is a very powerful statement. It means that two people have their faith combined, believing that the thing they are praying is so real, *it is as if they are touching it when they pray.* That means that if I want you to pray the prayer of agreement with me, you must know what I am in need of and we must both have faith for the full manifestation of the thing for which we are praying.

The prayer of agreement is very powerful. It is a divine principle of the universe and so it works for the righteous and the wicked. The Bible gives us an example of this in Genesis 11 when the people of the earth, all speaking the same language and in the same location began to build the Tower of Babel. But, when God came down and saw what they were doing He said:

"And the Lord came down to see the city and the tower, which the children of man had built. And the Lord said, "Behold, they are one people, and they have all one language, and this is only the beginning of what they will do. And nothing that they propose to do will now be impossible for them." (Genesis 11:5-6)

God saw that the people had located a universal principle. People of one language, in the same location having the same common purpose, will be able to accomplish anything they set out to do. The power of synergy is released and all of creation will take notice and move into position to bring to pass the desired intent. The Apostle Paul made a request to the Church at Rome for a prayer of agreement:

"Now I beseech you, brethren, for the Lord Jesus Christ's sake, and for the love of the Spirit, that ye strive together with me in your prayers to God for me; That I may be delivered from them that do not believe in Judaea; and that my service which I have for Jerusalem may be accepted of the saints;" (Romans 15:30-31)

This is a wonderful example to show us that the prayer of agreement is not just about flesh touching flesh. The prayer of agreement is a prayer of travail. Paul asked them to strive – to wrestle – in prayer to pray for him to be delivered from unbelievers and for his ministry service to be accepted. This is not a simple matter. The prayer of agreement is a warfare prayer.

The enemy knows how to use the power of agreement as a weapon against us. Indeed it is the agreement of the enemy that provokes the wrath of God to defend us. We have discussed the more than 40 men in Acts 23 who fasted to kill Paul and that God placed Paul's nephew in a position to reveal the plot. The agreement of the enemy against the righteous will release the hand of God to deliver the righteous. But, God will not take it lightly when the righteous comes into agreement with the enemy. It will provoke His wrath against us.

During the reign of Hezekiah, the king caused Judah to enter an agreement with the Assyrians for protection. But, God knows Satan very well. God knows that Satan is a bad business partner and that he will never show kindness to humanity. That is why God's counsel has already determined the end for the wicked. The Bible says:

> *"A righteous man regardeth the life of his beast: but the tender mercies of the wicked are cruel." (Proverbs 12:10)*

The tender mercies of the wicked are cruelty. When Hezekiah attempted to make a political alliance with Egypt, the Prophet Isaiah described God's wrath:

> *"Because ye have said, We have made a covenant with death, and with hell are we at agreement; when the overflowing scourge shall pass through, it shall not come unto us: for we have made lies our refuge, and under falsehood have we hid ourselves: And your covenant with death shall be disannulled, and your agreement with hell shall not stand; when the overflowing scourge shall pass through, then ye shall be trodden down by it." (Isaiah 28:15 & 18)*

The Lord likens the agreement with Egypt as an agreement with death, hell and the grave. But, He tells them the alliance will not stand because the devil is a liar! He tells them agreeing with the enemy will never produce favorable results for the righteous.

Beloved, the devil is really not trying to fight you. He knows he will not win because Jesus has already defeated Satan. The Bible says –

> *"And the seventy returned again with joy, saying, Lord, even the devils are subject unto us through thy name. And he said unto them, I beheld Satan as lightning fall from heaven. Behold, I give unto you power to tread on serpents and scorpions, and over all the power of the enemy: and nothing shall by any means hurt you. Notwithstanding in this rejoice not, that the spirits are subject unto you; but rather rejoice, because your names are written in heaven." (Luke 10:17-20)*

Satan has already been defeated and citizens of the Kingdom of God will always be able to bring his kingdom down. For this we know:

> *"And there was war in heaven: Michael and his angels fought against the dragon; and the dragon fought and his angels, and prevailed not; neither was their place found any more in heaven. And the great dragon was cast out, that old serpent, called the Devil, and Satan, which deceiveth the whole world: he was cast out into the earth, and his angels were cast out with him. And I heard a loud voice saying in*

heaven, Now is come salvation, and strength, and the kingdom of our God, and the power of his Christ: for the accuser of our brethren is cast down, which accused them before our God day and night. And they overcame him by the blood of the Lamb, and by the word of their testimony; and they loved not their lives unto the death. Therefore rejoice, ye heavens, and ye that dwell in them. Woe to the inhabiters of the earth and of the sea! for the devil is come down unto you, having great wrath, because he knoweth that he hath but a short time." (Revelation 12:7-12)

Satan's powers are limited and when we operate from the Throne Room perspective and deal with him in the realm of the spirit, he cannot win. So his best strategy is to keep you from praying at all.

If you start praying and he reacts, it is to get you to stop praying. He puts up a resistance to your prayers to get you to agree with him that it is not working for you. But, he is a liar and the master of deception.

When you study the battle between Hezekiah and the Assyrian king in 2 Kings 18 it is filled with the battle strategies of the enemy. He will twist your arm and as soon as you give in thinking he will stop twisting your arm, he will snap it off. He will then convince you that God will not help you because if you were going to receive help, he wouldn't have been able to snap your arm off to begin with. He will tell you to stop fighting and he will take it easy on you, but that you will have to go into captivity where he will take whatever you have left in possessions and kill you when he is finished. His mercies are tender cruelty. But, beloved God has given you a way out. Have faith in God. Never trust the enemy. Trust God alone.

It is the Prayer of Agreement that when we follow the principles above and execute the judgment written against Satan alongside other believers, we gain tremendous ground and win territory for the Lord Jesus Christ. Paul told the church to pray two things:

1. Deliver him from the wicked people in the city
2. Cause his message to be received by the saints

That is still the prayer of agreement we must pray for those who are called to bring the Good News to a lost and dying world. Pray in agreement with them that they will be delivered from wicked men and that their message of the Gospel of the Kingdom will be received.

Chapter Summary:

- We must be willing to abide daily in Christ to bear fruit in our lives

- Abiding is a major key to answered prayers

- To be *in Christ* is not the same as *abiding in Christ*. Salvation can be ours, but it is our choice daily to build our relationship with Christ through the fellowship of daily prayer.

- Abiding in Christ helps us to pray by Revelation and under the inspiration of the Holy Spirit.

- People all over the world in every religion (and even atheists) have a measure of faith and can pray the prayer of faith. The difference is who they expect to answer the prayer. Jesus tells us to "Have faith in God."

- Corporate Prayer is essential to build stamina in prayer. But, corporate prayer should not be used as a substitute for relationship building with Christ.

- Corporate Prayer should not be confused with the Prayer of Agreement

- The Prayer of Agreement is a warfare prayer. It is a travailing prayer. It must be prayed for those who are called to spread the message of the Gospel.

Chapter 13

Decreeing and Declaring

"The world does not need sermons; it needs a message. You can go to seminary and learn how to preach sermons, but you will have to go to God to get messages." – **Oswald J. Smith**

Prayer moves God to enforce His Word and bring to pass His original intent for mankind. My prayer for you is that the eyes of your understanding have been enlightened and your prayer life will never be the same. I want to leave you with two powerful keys: the key of declaration and the key of decrees.

Declarations

The word "declare" comes from the Hebrew *achvah*, meaning "to make known" or "to set forth an accounting." As it pertains to us spiritually, declare is an apostolic mandate of the church to set forth or make known the blessings of God – for a person, a family, a church, a nation, etc. When you, as a believer, pronounce through a declaration in prayer, you are enforcing the blessing, which the Spirit has already revealed.

That which we have seen and heard declare we unto you, that ye also may have fellowship with us: and truly our fellowship is with the Father, and with his Son Jesus Christ. And these things write we unto you, that your joy may be full. This then is the message which we have heard of him, and declare unto you, that God is light, and in him is no darkness at all. (1 John 1:3-5)

Prophetic declarations typically denote the blessings of the Lord and involve the enforcement of answered prayer. As seen in 1 John 1:3-5, the Apostles were declaring to the church the message and sure testimony of their eyewitness account of Jesus Christ. A declaration speaks forth and establishes the blessings and promises of God.

Throughout the Gospels, Jesus Christ used the word declare repeatedly to announce the message of the Kingdom of God. He declares a prophetic blessing to change the name of Peter:

And I declare to you that you are Peter, and that upon this Rock I will build my Church, and the might of Hades shall not triumph over it. (Matthew 16:18)

He teaches the disciples that when the Holy Spirit comes, He will announce and reveal Christ by declaration:

However when he, the Spirit of truth, has come, he will guide you into all truth, for he will not speak from himself; but whatever he hears, he will speak. He will declare to you things that are coming. He will glorify me, for he will take from what is mine, and will declare it to you. All things whatever the Father has are mine; therefore I said that he takes of mine, and will declare it to you." (John 16:13-15)

This prophetic declaration was confirmed when the Holy Spirit came on the Day of Pentecost. Scriptures say:

And in the day of the Pentecost being fulfilled, they were all with one accord at the same place, and there came suddenly out of the heaven a sound as of a bearing violent breath, and it filled all the house where they were sitting, and there appeared to them divided tongues, as it were of fire; it sat also upon each one of them, and they were all filled with the Holy Spirit, and began to speak with other tongues, according as the Spirit was giving them to declare. (Acts 2:1-4)

The Holy Spirit gave them *utterance or the ability to declare* as He gives us today when we declare that which we have seen and heard in times of prayer. That is using declarations correctly.

Declarations typically benefit the speaker and affect those he or she is speaking to. However, there are times when satanic declarations or wicked verdicts must be overturned. The Bible says:

> ***I will overturn, overturn, overturn, it: and it shall be no more, until he come whose right it is; and I will give it him. (Ezekiel 21:27)***

This means that a satanic verdict that is contrary to the Word of God and His prophetic declaration over the Righteous can be overturned. However, there are other rules of engagement.

When the righteous stretch forth their hand to sin – as we see happened in the Garden of Eden – the enemy is able to go beyond a mere declaration of evil intentions. Now, he is able to enact the decrees of judgment against us based on the sin. This is why we all still die, even though death has been defeated. The hope we have in Christ is this:

> ***For the law of the Spirit of life in Christ Jesus hath made me free from the law of sin and death. (Romans 8:2)***

I am free from the law of sin and death by a superior law. The superior sacrifice of the Blood of Jesus must be superimposed over the law of sin and death. This is not a declaration. This is when prophetic decrees are necessary.

Decrees

A decree is a very powerful weapon in the hands of authority. The Hebrew word for "decree" is *gazar* and it means to cut, to divide, or to separate. A decree is a pronouncement of judgment from an authority figure.

Prophetic decrees are predictive prophecies that resemble decrees by God determining the course of history. This is why they must be spoken in the realm of the Spirit as we are letting the Spirit pray through us. A decree has the power to stand for time and eternity. Prophetic decrees of blessing can be nullified by disobedience.

Predictive decrees are used both to bless and to punish. Sometimes predictive decrees to punish can be abrogated through repentance and averting punishment. The Prophet Zephaniah gave instructions on how to avert the decreed punishment of the Lord:

> *Gather yourselves together, yea, gather together, O nation not desired; Before the decree bring forth, before the day pass as the chaff, before the fierce anger of the Lord come upon you, before the day of the Lord's anger come upon you. Seek ye the Lord, all ye meek of the earth, which have wrought his judgment; seek righteousness, seek meekness: it may be ye shall be hid in the day of the Lord's anger. (Zephaniah 2:1-3)*

Your prayer can move God to show Mercy. But, there are some decrees that will require warfare. We see in the Book of Esther that Haman was able to get the king to make a decree that could not be overturned except by a counter-decree. The Bible says:

> *If it please the king, let it be written that they may be destroyed: and I will pay ten thousand talents of silver to the hands of those that have the charge of the business, to bring it into the king's treasuries. And the king took his ring from his hand, and gave it unto Haman the son of Hammedatha the Agagite, the Jews' enemy. And the king said unto Haman, The silver is given to thee, the people also, to do with them as it seemeth good to thee. (Esther 3:9-11)*

This was the judgment written against the Jews by their enemy, Haman. Once the king's ring sealed this decree, mere words could not overturn it. Not even the king could repeal the written law. He had to write a new law.

Even though Haman had been hung on his own gallows, his property given to Esther and his ring given to Mordecai, the wicked decree to annihilate the Jews still could not be overturned without a counter-decree.

And Esther spake yet again before the king, and fell down at his feet, and besought him with tears to put away the mischief of Haman the Agagite, and his device that he had devised against the Jews. Then the king held out the golden sceptre toward Esther. So Esther arose, and stood before the king, And said, If it please the king, and if I have favour in his sight, and the thing seem right before the king, and I be pleasing in his eyes, let it be written to reverse the letters devised by Haman the son of Hammedatha the Agagite, which he wrote to destroy the Jews which are in all the king's provinces. (Esther 8:3-5)

The king listened to Esther and because she had found favor, he gave her this advice:

Then the king Ahasuerus said unto Esther the queen and to Mordecai the Jew, Behold, I have given Esther the house of Haman, and him they have hanged upon the gallows, because he laid his hand upon the Jews. Write ye also for the Jews, as it liketh you, in the king's name, and seal it with the king's ring: for the writing which is written in the king's name, and sealed with the king's ring, may no man reverse. (Esther 8:7-8)

Here he tells her the judgment or decree of the king is final. No one can overrule the written judgment. The Word is powerful, my friend. The enemy is always trying to get you to break the commands of God so that he can execute the judgment written against you. This is why we pray:

Blotting out the handwriting of ordinances that was against us, which was contrary to us, and took it out of the way, nailing it to his cross; (Colossians 2:14) and

Can the prey be taken from the mighty, or the captives of a tyrant be rescued? For thus says the Lord: "Even the captives of the mighty shall be taken, and the prey of the tyrant be rescued, for I will contend with those who contend with you, and I will save your children. (Isaiah 49:24-25)

Beloved, God will rescue you by His hand of Mercy. But, when we are battling the enemy and standing in the gap for generations yet unborn, we must know the weapons of our warfare and the tactics of the enemy. The final judgment of the king read:

And he wrote in the king Ahasuerus' name, and sealed it with the king's ring, and sent letters by posts on horseback, and riders on mules, camels, and young dromedaries: Wherein the king granted the Jews which were in every city to gather themselves together, and to stand for their life, to destroy, to slay and to cause to perish, all the power of the people and province that would assault them, both little ones and women, and to take the spoil of them for a prey. (Esther 8:10-11)

Here we see that the verdict was not overturned. Just like the verdict of death that came as a result of sin, the Jews were subject to be assaulted because of the first decree. So, the counter decree doesn't overturn the first law. Instead, it gave them a weapon of defense that they would need to "stand for their life."

Beloved, that is where we are today. That is why we must pray strategic prayers if we are going to get the victory. We must pray. Daily prayer is required for daily triumph. Prayer moves God.

Chapter Summary:

- Prayer moves God to enforce His Word and bring to pass His original intent for mankind.

- The word "declare" comes from the Hebrew achvah, meaning "to make known" or "to set forth an accounting."

- Declarations are used to set forth or make known the blessings of God

- You are enforcing the blessing, which the Spirit has already revealed

- Satanic declarations or wicked verdicts can be overturned

- A decree is a very powerful weapon in the hands of authority. It is a pronouncement of judgment

- The Hebrew word for "decree" is gazar and it means to cut, to divide, or to separate.

- When it cannot be overturned, it must be overruled by a higher law or a counter-decree

- We enforce our Dominion Mandate using declarations and decrees under the inspiration of the Holy Spirit

- Prayer is a daily necessity for daily triumph.

For more from the Archbishop:

Prayer Summit International
www.prayersummitinternational.org

Action Chapel Prayer Cathedral
Spintex Road, Ghana, West Africa

SUNDAY MORNING SERVICES
7 AM - 9:30 AM
10 AM - 12:30 PM
EVENING SERVICE -
6 PM - 8:30 PM
WEDNESDAY (MIDWEEK) SERVICE:
6 PM - 8:30 PM
DOMINION HOUR (Thursdays):
9 AM - 12 NOON.
MORNING GLORY (Saturdays):
7 AM - 9:30 AM.
FIRM FOUNDATION SUNDAY SERVICES:
7 AM - 9:30 AM
10 AM - 12:30 PM
RELEVANCE SUNDAY SERVICE:
3 PM – 4:30PM.

For Action branches, fellowships, and other church activities, please call +233.302.745.000, or visit www.actionchapel.net

USA Branch Churches

Action Chapel Virginia, www.actionchapelva.org
Action Chapel Baltimore, www.actionchapelbaltimore.com
Action Worship Center Laurel, www.awclaurel.org

Printed in Great Britain
by Amazon